EAGLES

PETER R. MARCH

EAGLES

80 AIRCRAFT THAT MADE HISTORY WITH THE RAF

PETER R. MARCH

WEIDENFELD & NICOLSON
LONDON

First published in Great Britain in 1998
by Weidenfeld & Nicolson

Text copyright © Peter R. March 1998
The moral right of Peter R. March to be identified as the author of this work has been asserted in
accordance with the Copyright, Designs and Patents Act of 1988
Photographs © Royal Air Force Benevolent Fund Enterprises
Design and layout copyright © Weidenfeld & Nicolson, 1998

A CIP catalogue record for this book is available from the British Library
ISBN 0 297 82482 1

Designed by: Paul Cooper
Set in: M Bembo
Printed in: Italy

Weidenfeld & Nicolson
The Orion Publishing Group Ltd
5 Upper Saint Martin's Lane
London WC2H 9EA

CONTENTS

The 80th anniversary of the Royal Air Force is a significant landmark in the history of the Service. Looking forward from its inception in 1918 few, if any, would have believed the almost incredible advances in aircraft technology to be made over the following decades.

Throughout these 80 years the members of the Royal Air Force have distinguished themselves, whether in time of war, or as peace-keepers, or as humanitarians providing food aid, or in many other types of operations in the cause of freedom and in the relief of distress.

This book of fine illustrations is a tribute to the Service and provides a record of eighty of the most notable aircraft that have served the Royal Air Force so well during its long and illustrious history. At the same time I hope the book will provide much-needed additional income for the Royal Air Force Benevolent Fund, whose resources are constantly being called on, particularly by those who fought in the Second World War and are now in need of the Fund's help.

HRH The Duke of Kent, KG
President
The Royal Air Force Benevolent Fund

THE EAGLE SOARS

The Royal Air Force was formed on 1 April 1918 by the amalgamation of the Royal Flying Corps and the Royal Naval Air Service. Despite early reservations that flying machines would never have a role in warfare, by the end of World War I it was clear that these were misplaced. In June 1918, the Independent Air Force was formed with one fighter squadron and nine bomber squadrons to operate by day and night against German industrial targets and airfields. It was the first time that an air force had been created to operate without reference or subordination to Army or Navy commands.

By the end of World War I, the new Service comprised 22,647 aircraft and 103 airships in 383 squadrons and fifteen flights. Personnel amounted to over 300,000, of whom some 25,000 were women. Yet, in less than eighteen months, the RAF had dwindled to twenty-five operational squadrons and fewer than 30,000 personnel. Under Major General Trenchard, Chief of the Air Staff, the RAF fought for survival. Its position was strengthened in 1919 with the introduction of the titles Secretary of State and Under Secretary of State for Air and by the creation of its own rank titles.

Trenchard, who gained the title of 'Father of the RAF', foresaw that its foundations had to be secured on the grounds of quality and on a framework which could be rapidly expanded when necessary. This far-sighted approach saw the creations of the RAF College Cranwell in 1920, the RAF Aircraft Apprentice School of Technical Training at Halton in 1922 and the RAF Staff College for senior officers at Andover in the same year.

The majority of the RAF's few flying squadrons were then based in the Near and Middle East. Trenchard contended that the vast areas of desert and mountains within the British Empire could be controlled far more easily and economically from the air than by the traditional methods of garrisons on the ground. This theory was first put into practice in early 1920, when a force of twelve DH9 bombers and 219 officers and men was sent to Somaliland to deal with a significant rebel force. After several bombing raids, the remnants of the rebels surrendered to the Somaliland Camel Corps.

There were no RAF casualties and the action demonstrated how air power could be used to police large tracts of land. Following that success, the military control of the whole of Iraq was subsequently handed over to the RAF.

Despite its small size, the RAF was at the forefront of progress throughout the 1920s and 1930s. Records were set over distances which may seem short by modern-day standards but, in the days of single-engined, open cockpit biplanes flying over uncharted lands, were no mean achievement. In 1927, the RAF received its first all-metal fighter when the Armstrong Whitworth Siskin IIIA entered service with No 41 Squadron. In the same year, the RAF won the Schneider Trophy race for seaplanes with a Supermarine S5, the same aircraft setting up a new 100km closed circuit speed record of 283.67 mph. Supermarine seaplanes won the Schneider Trophy twice more, thus ensuring its permanent retention by Britain. In 1937, a Bristol 138 established a new height record of 53,937 feet.

It was not until 1934 that events in Europe gave rise to the RAF Expansion Scheme which called for the number of Home Defence squadrons to be increased to seventy-five. Modernization was badly needed: at the Royal Review of 1935, over 350 aircraft were present, all of them biplanes. In December 1937, the RAF's first single-seat low-wing monoplane fighter, the Hurricane, entered service with No 111 Squadron, followed in June 1938 by the 355 mph Spitfire. These fighters, together with more modern bomber types such as the Blenheim, Wellington and the American Hudson, ensured that the RAF had a nucleus of effective aircraft at the outbreak of World War II.

During World War II, air power played a vital part in achieving victory. In 1940, victory in the Battle of Britain ensured the survival of the United Kingdom and co-operation in the Western Desert between the RAF and the Army provided the framework for all future tactical air operations. Yet the primary role of the RAF was that envisaged in 1918 – strategic bombing. The price was high: of a total of 70,253 RAF personnel killed in action, 55,573 were Bomber Command aircrew.

With the advent of the nuclear age in the 1950s, the RAF's V-force of four-engined jet bombers became responsible for the UK's nuclear deterrent. Between 1958 and 1963, the V-force was supplemented by sixty Thor ICBMs. The Ballistic Missile Early Warning Station at RAF Fylingdales was capable of giving four minutes warning of any attack. Well within this time, the RAF's bombers on Quick Reaction Alert would have been airborne in retaliation, some carrying the Blue Steel stand-off bomb.

From 1968 onwards, the Commands were restructured as a result of the Government's decision to withdraw British forces from east of Suez with the exception of Hong Kong. In 1969, the maintenance of the nuclear deterrent passed to the Royal Navy's Polaris submarine force. The RAF continued to be responsible for tactical nuclear operations until 1998, and the defence of the home base, as well as the rapid reinforcement of remaining overseas bases.

Twice within the last eleven years the RAF has been called upon to exercise the flexibility of air power in the face of aggression. During the recapture of the Falkland Islands in 1982, the RAF deployed offensive, defensive and support forces over 8000 miles from the home base. RAF Harriers provided offensive firepower alongside their Royal Navy counterparts operating from ships and temporary shore bases. After the loss of the Atlantic Conveyor, the sole surviving Chinook helicopter played a major role in the support of the land forces; and Vulcans flew strategic bombing missions from Ascension Island, at that time the longest raids ever carried out. Major factors in the success of the operation were the massive efforts of both the air transport and the air-to-air refuelling forces in maintaining the logistic chain from the UK to Ascension Island and on down to the South Atlantic.

In August 1990, Iraq invaded Kuwait. Within forty-eight hours of the British Government's decision to send forces to the Gulf, a squadron of Tornado F3s arrived in Saudi Arabia and flew their first operational patrol only two hours later. They were joined after two days by a squadron of Jaguar ground-attack aircraft together with Nimrods for maritime patrol and VC10 tankers. There is little doubt that such prompt reaction by the Coalition forces deterred further aggression by Iraq.

At peak strength, the RAF had 158 aircraft and some 5,500 regular and reserve personnel in theatre, supported by the Air Transport Force. Air supremacy was achieved by the end of the first week of the campaign to enforce the UN resolutions. The Iraqi Air Force had either fled or been trapped on its damaged airfields. The 1000-hour air war enabled the ground forces to complete their campaign in one hundred hours without fear of opposition from the air.

Although direct hostilities were soon over, the RAF has had a continuing presence in the Gulf, policing the No-Fly Zones over Iraq from bases in Turkey and Saudi Arabia. Further crises have taken additional aircraft, such as the Harrier GR7s on board HMS *Invincible* and HMS *Illustrious*, during the winter 1997–8, into the area. Nearer to home the conflict in the former Yugoslavia kept the RAF's Hercules squadrons busy with relief flights into Sarajevo, the Support Helicopter Force have assisted UN and NATO ground forces and Harriers, Jaguars and Tornados have been heavily involved, along with E-3D Sentries and VC10 and Tristar tankers in patrolling the No-Fly Zones.

While all this has been taking place through the nineties the RAF has been reduced in manpower, aircraft, bases and the command structure has been rationalized. This has put greater pressure on the two key elements, the RAF's personnel and the equipment they are given, to meet the varied and constantly widening tasks to which the Service has to respond. In this, its eightieth year, the RAF is facing yet further rationalization to meet the challenges of an ever changing world in which air power continues to hold the key to global security. With eighty years of solid achievement behind it, the Royal Air Force looks forward to the new millennium with justifiable pride but no small amount of trepidation.

PETER R. MARCH

WORLD WAR I

BRISTOL F2B FIGHTER

The tragic losses of Royal Flying Corps airmen in the early days of World War I caused an outcry and this resulted in the War Office giving wider recognition to the designs of private aircraft firms, rather than just relying on those from the Royal Aircraft Factory. Designed by the Bristol Aeroplane Company, the two-seat Type 96, better known as the F2B Fighter (or 'Brisfit'), was produced in 1916. It had good structural strength, single-seat combat manoeuvrability and performance, plus the bonus of a rear gun.

Unlike the majority of the aircraft they were given to fly to war in 1914-18, the Bristol Fighter received nothing but praise from its aircrew. Few (if indeed any) demurred from this tribute, recorded

Right: The Bristol F2B Fighter like this Mk III Army Co-operation version, flew with Army Co-operation squadrons at home and abroad through the 1920s.

Above: In the great German offensive of April 1918, the Bristol Fighter squadrons in France played a major part in stopping the advancing infantry, flying almost at ground level with guns blazing, blasting the enemy batteries with bombs.

by Major Oliver Stewart MC. Another pilot commented, 'The Bristol Fighter should be spoken of in terms of the heroes of classic mythology. It was, in the fullest sense, a hero after their pattern – a fighter by name, inclination and aptitude. The pilot could enter a dogfight and turn almost as quickly and in almost as small a radius as the best single-seater.'

When the RAF was formed on 1 April 1918, the 'Brisfit' was in service with some thirty squadrons at

1918

home and abroad. It was a Bristol Fighter of No 22 Squadron that made the first flight of the new Service, when it took off from Vert Galand at dawn on that historic day. When the production of new aircraft under wartime contracts ceased in September 1919, no less than 4500 Bristol Fighters had been built for the RFC/RAF. Nearly 400 more were assembled in 1920 and many later reconditioned to re-enter service. The 'Brisfit' continued to serve with the RAF, mainly on policing duties overseas, until June 1932.

POWERPLANT: One 205kW (275hp) Rolls-Royce Falcon III piston-engine
SPAN: 11.96m (39ft 3in); **LENGTH:** 7.87m (25ft 10in)
MAX SPEED: 202km/h (125mph)
TYPICAL ARMAMENT: One 0.303in Vickers gun fixed on top centreline, single or twin 0.303in Lewis on Scarff ring on rear cockpit; provision for up to twelve 9kg (20lb) bombs
FIRST AIRCRAFT FLOWN: 9 September 1916
ENTERED RFC SERVICE: March 1917 (No 48 Squadron)
LAST RAF SERVICE: June 1932 (Mk IV, No 6 Squadron).

Left: Built in 1918 at Brislington, Bristol by the British & Colonial Aeroplane Company, this Bristol Fighter F2B Mk II was first flown on 15 June and delivered to the RAF in July 1918. It survived in storage until after World War II, was restored by the Bristol Aeroplane Company at Filton in 1951 and remains active today with the Shuttleworth Trust.

AVRO 504K

esign work on the Avro 504 commenced in November 1912 and, for a pre-1914 type, it had an almost unprecedented production run of twenty years. During this time it appeared in a great many variants, having proved to be ahead of most contemporary types in terms of design and performance. All versions featured the distinctive ash skid between the wheels to prevent it nosing over on the ground.

The 504K was the most numerous and widely-used of the series, and differed from previous models in having a universal engine mounting to take a variety of powerplants, especially Le Rhône and Clerget rotary engines. The last 504K to be built was not delivered until 1927 – the total of all 504 variants being 8970.

In 1918, a number of 504Ks, modified as single-seaters, but armed with a Lewis gun on a Foster mounting above the wing, were specifically introduced to replace the ageing BE2Cs with the Home Defence squadrons. Five squadrons, equipped with a total of 226 Avro 504s were still flying at the time of the Armistice – together with 2267 aircraft in use at Flying Training Schools.

Commander Peter Bagley recalled his early experience with the 504K, 'Pilots were taught engine handling before any flight manoeuvres because the rotary engine had to be either shut off completely for landings or use made of a blip switch fitted on top of the stick – a solid wooden type like a walking stick. The engine was prone to coughing and to cutting out when throttled back, and could not be restarted until

Right: This RAF Avro 504K photographed flying in the 1920s shows the rear-seat passenger climbing out onto the port wing. It is believed that he fell to his death, when he slipped from the wing shortly afterwards. The RAF official photograph was found stored at RAF Thorney Island in 1975.

1918

POWERPLANT: One 82kW (110hp) Le Rhône, 97kW (130hp) Clerget or 75kW (100hp) Monosoupape rotary engine
SPAN: 10.97m (36ft); LENGTH: 8.96m (29ft 5in)
MAX SPEED: 153km/h (95mph)
ACCOMMODATION: Two seats in tandem
FIRST AIRCRAFT FLOWN: 1918
ENTERED RAF SERVICE: 1918
LAST RAF SERVICE: March 1933.

the fuel lever had been shut and a wait of eight seconds had gone by.'

The 504K remained in service with the RAF as the standard equipment at the Central Flying School and Nos 1 to 5 Flying Training Schools, until the arrival of the Lynx-engined 504N in 1927. Avro 504s flown by instructors from the CFS and Flying Training Schools were a regular feature of the annual RAF Air Displays at Hendon in the 1920s.

Left: This very realistic replica Avro 504K, built by AJD Engineering in 1993 has the distinctive ash skid between the main wheels.

Above: Still airworthy in 1998, this Avro 504K was built at Manchester by A V Roe & Co Ltd and served with the RAF until 1931. After World War II it was restored to flying condition by the Bristol Aeroplane Co at Filton, presented to the Shuttleworth Trust, and now flies regularly at Old Warden.

De HAVILLAND DH9/DH9A

Although designed by Airco, forerunner of de Havilland, the DH9A was built by a number of other British manufacturers, particularly Westland at Yeovil, who had already built the DH4 on which the DH9 had been based. As the Rolls-Royce Eagle, the intended engine, was in such demand, Westland opted for the American Liberty engine.

Westland Chief Test Pilot Major Laurence Openshaw recalled, 'The fuselage was modified to accept the new powerplant and other improvements made. When air-tested there was little doubt that the resulting DH9A was fast, and indeed proved fast enough in service to fly over enemy territory without fighter escort. It became the outstanding strategic bomber aircraft of World War I and brought Westland recognition as a capable design and construction organization.'

The 'Ninak' as the DH9A was popularly known,

had a very long service life, being introduced during the last six months of WWI and remaining with RAF units until the early 1930s. Operating in France from August 1918, the DH9As were effective in daylight raids on German towns, and by the Armistice there were four squadrons operating the type.

POWERPLANT: One 298kW (400hp) Liberty 12A in-line piston engine
SPAN: 14.0m (46ft 0in); **Length:** 9.14m (30ft 0in)
MAX SPEED: 183km/h (114mph)
TYPICAL ARMAMENT: One Vickers gun forward and one Lewis gun aft; max bomb load 205kg (450lb)
FIRST AIRCRAFT FLOWN: 1917
ENTERED RAF SERVICE: 19 August 1918 (No 110 Squadron)
LAST RAF SERVICE: 1931.

Below: This tropicalized version of the DH9A, with an additional radiator under the nose, was the mainstay of the RAF in Iraq and the North West Frontier in the 1920s.

Above: Built by the Aircraft Manufacturing Co Ltd (Airco) this DH9A had the name 'Wizard', here flying over the Ctesiphon Arch in the Middle East.

Postwar, the last new-build aircraft was delivered to the RAF on 17 May 1927. Many DH9As were rebuilt or renovated and returned to the RAF, becoming the standard equipment with home-based day bomber squadrons until the arrival of the Fairey Fawn. Overseas it was the mainstay of squadrons until replaced by the Wapiti and Fairey IIIF. The 'Ninak' was widely used by Flying Training Schools and was a noted performer at Hendon RAF Displays.

In Iraq and on the North West Frontier the tropicalized version became a general purpose aircraft equipped with an additional radiator under the nose and an additional fuel tank. Here it became one of the first aircraft to become engaged on policing duties, and when working over difficult terrain, far from regular support, they often carried spare wheels, water, tents and bedding on the sides of the fuselage or between the undercarriage struts.

HANDLEY PAGE V/1500

The Handley Page V/1500, known as the 'Bloody Paralyser' and 'Super Handley' was the largest British bomber of World War I and with four engines was designed to bring Berlin within range of RAF bases in East Anglia. It must be regarded as the RAF's first practical strategic bomber, designed to strike targets from home bases, but the war finished before any could be used operationally. It was too large for the post-war RAF and despite an initial production order for 210 only a quarter of these were actually built and flown.

The V/1500's engines were mounted in tandem pairs between the wings, outboard of the fuselage. The type saw only limited post-war service with the RAF, gradually being replaced by the

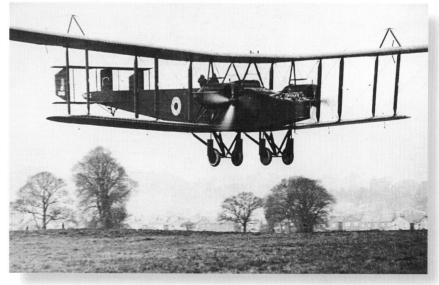

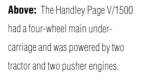

somewhat inferior, twin-engined Vickers Vimy. No 166 Squadron received three V/1500s at Bircham Newton in October 1918 and these aircraft were bombed up and ready to make a raid on Berlin when the war ended early in the following month.

A V/1500 was used to make the first through flight from England to India. Taking off on 13 December 1918, the aircraft flew via Rome, Malta, Cairo and Baghdad reaching Karachi on 30 December. It encountered a series of problems *en route* that were largely dealt with by the three mechanics carried on the aircraft, but despite their efforts it arrived at Karachi with two of its engines out of action. The V/1500 was used, in May 1919, to make a bomb attack on Kabul during the problems in Afghanistan. Remaining based at Bircham Newton, the V/1500s of No 166 Squadron were handed over to No 274 Squadron in May 1919, the last unit to operate the big bomber.

After an abortive attempt to make the first transatlantic flight in 1919, having been beaten by Alcock and Brown in a Vimy, the V/1500's last

POWERPLANT: Four 280kW (375hp) Rolls-Royce Eagle VIII in-line piston engines
SPAN: 38.40m (126ft 0in); Length: 19.51m (64ft 0in)
MAX SPEED: 159km/h (99mph)
TYPICAL ARMAMENT: Single Lewis gun in nose, dorsal, ventral and tail positions; max bomb load 3,402kg (7500lb)
FIRST AIRCRAFT FLOWN: May 1918
ENTERED RAF SERVICE: October 1918 (No 166 Squadron)
LAST RAF SERVICE: July 1920

appearance in public was at the RAF Display at Hendon on 3 July 1920, when three demonstrated a formation take-off.

Below: Based in East Anglia, No 27 Group's Handley Page V/1500 four-engined bombers were ready to make their first raid on Berlin when the Armistice intervened.

Above: The Handley Page V/1500 had a four-wheel main under-carriage and was powered by two tractor and two pusher engines.

Left: The Handley Page V/1500's last appearance in public was at the RAF Tournament at Hendon in July 1920, when the leading aircraft was flown by Sholto Douglas (later Marshal of the Royal Air Force Lord Douglas of Kirtleside).

BETWEEN THE WARS

AW SISKIN

Right: Armstrong Whitworth Siskin IIIA photographed on 11 August 1930. It was officially captioned 'Preparing for "Aerial War" - aerial manoeuvres between "Redland" and "Blueland" commencing tomorrow'.

The Armstrong Whitworth Siskin, in its developed form, was the mainstay of the RAF's biplane fighter inventory for the second half of the 1920s. The Air Ministry's policy of ordering all-metal aircraft only, forced Armstrong Siddeley to redesign the Siskin after several composite metal and wood aircraft had been built. The transition to metal construction did nothing to improve the appearance of the aircraft, that featured a somewhat angular outline with seemingly little regard paid to streamlining. The pilot sat just behind the top wing with his eyes roughly level with the trailing edge, and his view upward and forward was good. The long-travel undercarriage was a mass of struts, but was very rugged.

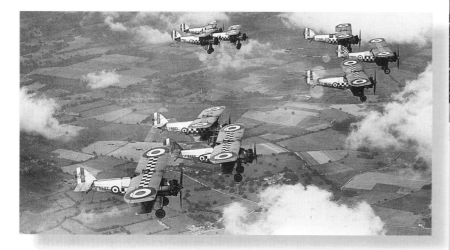

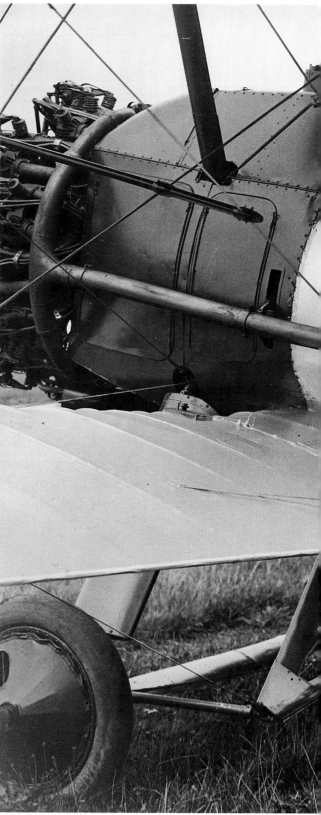

Above: A formation of nine Siskin IIIAs of No 43 Squadron. With a supercharged engine it had a commendable maximum speed of 156mph and a service ceiling of over 27,000ft.

POWERPLANT: One 242kW (325hp) Armstrong Siddeley Jaguar III radial engine (MkIII)
SPAN: 9.80m (32ft 2in); Length: 7.72m (25ft 4in)
MAX SPEED: 251km/h (156mph)
TYPICAL ARMAMENT: Two synchronised 0.303in Vickers machine guns in the upper nose decking; provision to carry up to four 9kg (20lb) bombs under the lower wings
FIRST AIRCRAFT FLOWN: 7 May 1923 (Mk III)
ENTERED RAF SERVICE: May 1924 (Mk III, No 41 Squadron)
LAST RAF SERVICE: October 1932 (Mk IIIA, No 56 Squadron).

A total of 485 Siskins, of all marks, was produced and it represented a landmark in the history of the RAF in that it was the first aircraft with all-metal structure to serve in quantity. Although slightly underpowered, the Siskin III proved to be very popular in RAF service. Some of the earlier versions were subsequently converted as two-seat trainers and these served at the RAF College, Cranwell, the Armament & Gunnery School and various Flying Training Schools.

Major Oliver Stewart, test pilot, writer and later Farnborough Air Show commentator, was one of the select few to test the original Siskin. He recalled, 'The aeroplane was extremely easy to fly, and it is probable that it was, up to that time, the easiest single-seat fighter to enter RAF service. In the past, single-seater fighters had been quick, snappy, short-tempered and sometimes vicious. But the Siskin was gentle, easy-going, calm and good tempered – a marked contrast to previous machines. In the air the Siskin was amenable to discipline and would do loops, rolls and spins graciously – if not quickly. The outlook was markedly good and the cockpit arrangements comfortable. It was an awkward looking machine – a great uncouth brute of a thing, but with a heart of gold.'

Above: A Siskin IIIA, as flown by No 43 Squadron at RAF Tangmere from June 1928 to June 1931.

VICKERS VIRGINIA

A large biplane, which in construction differed little from the Vickers Vimy, the unremarkable Virginia was designed and developed in the closing stages of World War I. It became the backbone of the RAF's heavy night-bomber squadrons in the inter-war years, remaining in service from 1924 until the mid-1930s. When production ended a total of 124 had been built. Apart from playing a vital role in the operational development of what was to become RAF Bomber Command, many Virginias continued to be used for parachute dropping and test purposes as late as 1941.

The Virginia was excessively tiring to fly and extremely slow with a bomb load of just 1364kg (3000lb). At no time during its service could it have reached a target more than fifty miles inside Germany, carrying anything but a meagre bomb load, from

RAF bases in eastern England. Yet it was one of the RAF's principal heavy bombers during the inter-war years of 'rearmament' against a fast-expanding, modern Luftwaffe.

In flight the Virginia tended to 'hunt' continuously in yaw and pitch, for which no adequate trimming device was ever provided. Keeping the bomber on an even keel imposed an enormous physical workload on the pilot, while giving the remainder of the crew a thoroughly uncomfortable flight. Night flying was somewhat hazardous for the less experienced pilot. Later marks introduced a gunner's position at the rear end of the fuselage, made possible by lengthening the nose to balance the centre of gravity, and widening the tail to improve stability.

In the mid-1920s No 58 (Bomber) Squadron was the first to receive a full complement of thirteen

Virginias. Command of this Squadron passed to thirty-three year old Squadron Leader Arthur Travers Harris who was to become Marshal of the Royal Air Force Sir Arthur Harris, the controversial Commander-in-Chief of Bomber Command from 1942 to 1945.

Below: A Vickers Virginia IV, converted to a Mk VII and then used in flight-refuelling experiments as a Mk X, seen here refuelling a Westland Wapiti.

POWERPLANT: Two 432kW (580hp) Napier Lion VB piston engines
Span: 26.71m (87ft 8in); Length: 18.99m (62ft 4in)
MAX SPEED: 158km/h (98mph)
TYPICAL ARMAMENT: One Lewis gun in nose and twin Lewis guns in tail; max bomb load 1364kg (3000lb)
FIRST AIRCRAFT FLOWN: 24 November 1922
ENTERED RAF SERVICE: 6 June 1924 (Mk III, No 7 Squadron)
LAST RAF SERVICE: 1941 (Mk X, Home Aircraft Depot).

Below and previous: No 500 Squadron was a Special Reserve unit, with half regular and half reserve personnel for its Virginias, which were operated from RAF Manston from March 1931 to January 1936. This example is named *City of Canterbury*.

FAIREY IIIF

Above: Fairey IIIF floatplanes of No 47 Squadron moored on the River Nile at Khartoum. The IIIFs were operated on floats for three months of the year.

The Fairey IIIA and B appeared in the year that the RAF was born, and the last of this line, the IIIF, left the service in 1935, just four years before the outbreak of World War II. It is surprising that an aircraft with such a long lineage should never have had a name - indeed, the Air Ministry, annoyed with Fairey, asked, 'Why do they not respond to requests to submit a name?' The Ministry proposed Salmon or Griffin, but it continued to the end as the Fairey IIIF.

In March 1927 four IIIFs made a Cairo-Cape-Cairo record-breaking flight. Air Commander C R Samson, Chief of Staff, Middle East, led the flight and on return said, 'This flight over the difficult 11,000 mile route was remarkable because, using new aircraft with which the RAF had no previous experience, it was completed virtually without trouble and to a pre-arranged schedule.' It was built in larger numbers (622, of which 340 went to the Fleet Air Arm) than any other military aircraft between the wars. The rugged biplane entered RAF squadron service at Khartoum in December 1927 when No 47 Squadron replaced its Bristol Fighters. At home the Fairey IIIF was used as a day bomber, replacing DH9As. No 202

Below: A Fairey IIIF of No 8 Squadron being hand refuelled at Salalah airfield whilst based at Khormaksar, Aden between January 1928 to April 1935.

Squadron based in Malta flew the twin-float seaplane version from July 1930 until they were replaced by Supermarine Scapas in August 1935.

Whilst flying in a IIIF, HRH The Prince of Wales was 'attacked' by Siskin fighters during the 1930 air exercises – an incident widely reported in the press.

Right: Several Fairey IIIFs, including K1115 seen here, were used by the RAF's No 24 (Communications) Squadron for carrying people on state journeys. They were modified with special passenger accommodation.

The IIIF transported several distinguished politicians on government business – Prime Minister Ramsay McDonald flew in one as a passenger to the Disarmament Conference in 1932.

POWERPLANT: One 425kW (570hp) Napier Lion XIA in-line piston engine
SPAN: 13.9m (45ft 9in); **Length:** 10.4m (36ft 9in)
MAX SPEED: 193km/h (120mph)
TYPICAL ARMAMENT: One Vickers gun and one Lewis gun; max bomb load 227kg (500lb)
FIRST AIRCRAFT FLOWN: 19 March 1926
ENTERED RAF SERVICE: March 1927 (No 47 Squadron)
LEFT RAF SERVICE: December 1935 (No 45 Squadron).

BRISTOL BULLDOG

The Bulldog was one of the best of the 'silver' biplanes to fly with the Royal Air Force during the 1930s. Though less graceful in appearance than contemporary Hawker designs with Rolls-Royce in-line engines, the radial-engined Bulldog lived up to its namesake as being a 'pugnacious and aggressive fighter'. It served with ten of the then-existing thirteen RAF fighter squadrons in the early 1930s, and enthralled crowds at Hendon and elsewhere with its aerobatic qualities. Its high tensile steel framework and fabric covering gave it exceptional strength. The Bulldog was fast, manoeuvrable and adequately armed.

Many of those who flew Bulldogs in the mid-1930s were destined to be fighting air battles in more modern aircraft in the Battle of Britain. It provided a hard core of excellent squadron and flight commanders in the crucial early months of World War II. The legendary Douglas Bader lost his legs whilst carrying out low-level aerobatics in a Bulldog at Woodley in 1931. For some years Bulldogs comprised about seventy per cent of the UK's fighter defences.

POWERPLANT: One 365kW (490ph) Bristol Jupiter VIIF radial piston engine
SPAN: 10.30m (33ft 10in); Length: 7.7m (25ft 2in)
MAX SPEED: 280km/h (174mph)
TYPICAL ARMAMENT: Two 0.303 in Vickers machine guns in fuselage sides. Provision for underwing racks for four 9.1kg (20lb) bombs
FIRST AIRCRAFT FLOWN: 17 May 1927
ENTERED RAF SERVICE: May 1929 (No 3 Squadron)
LAST RAF SERVICE: September 1937 (No 3 Squadron).

Right: Bristol Bulldogs of No 3 Squadron based at Kenley performing formation aerobatics with coloured smoke-trails at Hendon during the RAF display in July 1935.

Above: The Bristol Bulldog remained the most widely-used RAF fighter until 1936. During the Abyssinian crisis Bulldogs of No 3 Squadron were sent to the Sudan.

Flight Lieutenant (later Sir) Harry Broadhurst recalls his days with No 19(F) Squadron, 'At the beginning of 1934, I was posted to command "A" Flight equipped with Bulldogs. Whilst there, I led the Flight in aerobatics for the Hendon Air Display, also did a solo aerobatic display. The most spectacular combination was leading a flight of five, demonstrating aerobatics with smoke. In my day you pumped the stuff into the exhaust and the smoke came out on each side of the aircraft cockpit.'

WESTLAND WAPITI

It was said by many that the Wapiti 'held the Empire together' in the inter-war years. At the end of 1926 the Air Ministry had come to the conclusion that, however short of funds it was, it could no longer delay at least a token attempt to replace some of its outmoded aircraft. They were required, primarily, to supersede the DH9A that had given such valuable service. The Westland Wapiti was selected, and the initial contract was for twenty-five general-purpose aircraft. Little did they know that the company was eventually to build 563 of these multi-purpose biplanes. The Wapiti gave long and reliable service to the RAF on the North-West Frontier of India, where it equipped eight squadrons, and over the deserts of Iraq with three squadrons. In addition, they were the mainstay of the Auxiliary Air Force, equipping ten day-bomber squadrons.

Major Laurence Openshaw took the Wapiti for its maiden flight in the spring of 1927 and wrote, 'Again, it was Sunday morning and many employees came to watch. All felt this was a crucial day affecting their continued employment. We knew that five rival firms were competing for orders with their own versions of aircraft to the same specification. I climbed aboard with clinking parachute which the firm had at last purchased. With a commonplace machine there could be trouble – and there was! The rudder hardly worked at all! On investigation it was discovered that the fuselage had been drawn two feet shorter than intended. When rectified, we sent the machine to Martlesham so that the Air Ministry's RAF pilots could decide whether it was good enough.'

Although the Wapiti had long been retired by the home-based Auxiliary Air force squadrons

Below: No 31 Squadron was based at Mosul in Iraq from 1929 to 1936, shortly after the RAF was given responsibility for the new Kingdom of Iraq. The squadron was equipped with the Westland Wapiti IIA at that time.

1929

POWERPLANT: One 410kW (550hp) Bristol Jupiter
VIII or VIIIF radial piston engine (Mk IIA)
SPAN: 14.14m (46ft 5in); Length: 9.65m (31ft 8in)
MAX SPEED: 217km/h (135mph)
TYPICAL ARMAMENT: One fixed Vickers gun forward
and one Lewis gun aft; max bomb load 264kg (580lb)
FIRST AIRCRAFT FLOWN: 7 March 1927
ENTERED RAF SERVICE: July 1928 (No 84 Squadron)
LAST RAF SERVICE: October 1940 (No 27 Squadron).

(Nos 607/608 Squadrons in January 1937), there
were still eighty-four Wapiti IIAs in service in India in
September 1939. They were finally replaced by
Hawker Harts with No 5 Squadron in June 1940 and
No 27 Squadron in October 1940.

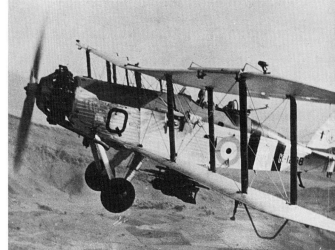

Left: For nineteen years No 55
Squadron formed part of the peace-
keeping force in Iraq, taking part in
various operations against raiding
tribesmen. The Squadron operated
the Westland Wapiti from February
1930 to March 1937, a formation of
three seen here over the River Tigris.

Above: Westland Wapiti IIA of No
5 Squadron. This Squadron served
in India for a quarter of a century
from 1920, being equipped with
Wapitis from 1931 until 1940.

HAWKER FURY

The most elegant biplane fighter of all those supplied to the inter-war RAF, the Fury was remembered with much affection by all who flew it. At the 1931 RAF Display, three Fury Is of No 43 Squadron gave a polished display of aerobatics – the first of many Hendon appearances where the machine became a star performer. The late Owen Thetford in his book *Aircraft of the Royal Air Force Since 1918* remarked, '...it was light and sensitive on the controls, had a fast climb, and was quite unsurpassed for aerobatic prowess'. In 1933, No 25 Squadron delighted Hendon spectators with tied-together aerobatics.

One of the last of the biplane and fixed under-carriage fighters of the RAF, the Fury I served with three home fighter squadrons (Nos 1, 25 and 43 Squadrons) until the arrival of the Hurricane and Spitfire. It epitomized the small biplane interceptor, sacrificing range and all-weather equipment for outstanding flight performance – it was delightful to

fly and 30mph faster than larger contemporary fighters, with an outstanding rate of climb. One Fury pilot said, 'It is the most beautiful biplane ever built', and others, 'That it was the most perfect fighter that could be built.' Production of the Fury I totalled 117 by 1935, when it was succeeded by the improved Fury II. Fitted with a 640hp Rolls-Royce Kestrel VI engine in place of the Mk I's 525hp Kestrel IIS, spatted wheels and other refinements, the Fury II was eight per cent faster and had a thirty-four per cent better rate of climb.

First flown in 1936, Fury IIs were delivered to Nos 25, 41, 73 and 87 Squadrons as single-seat interceptor fighters as well as to a number of RAF Flying Training Schools, the RAF College, Cranwell and the Central Flying School. As late as September 1939 nearly fifty Fury IIs remained active with various training units.

POWERPLANT: One 391kW (525hp) Rolls-Royce Kestrel II in-line piston engine (Fury Mk I)
SPAN: 9.14m (30ft 0in); Length: 4.3m (26ft 0.5in)
MAX SPEED: 339km/h (207mph)
TYPICAL ARMAMENT: Twin, synchronized Vickers guns
FIRST AIRCRAFT FLOWN: 25 March 1931
ENTERED RAF SERVICE: May 1931 (No 43 Squadron)
LAST RAF SERVICE: Late 1939.

Left: Eight Hawker Fury Is in echelon from No 1 Squadron. They were the RAF's official aerobatic team in 1937-1938, performing at Hendon and other major flying displays.

Right: No 43 Squadron at RAF Tangmere was one of the first to receive the Hawker Fury. Here is a brand-new Fury I on delivery in May 1931. It served until the squadron converted to Hurricanes at the end of 1938.

De HAVILLAND TIGER MOTH

Right: During the war years most RAF pilots were trained on Tiger Moths, one of the greatest biplane trainers of all time.

The DH82A Tiger Moth provided initial flying experience for most wartime RAF and Commonwealth pilots and it remained in RAF service as a basic trainer for over fifteen years, and with the University Air Squadrons until 1955. The main users were the overseas Elementary Flying Training Schools (EFTS) and at home the civilian-operated Elementary and Reserve Flying Training Schools. In addition to training, it was given some unlikely jobs early in the war, flying patrols searching for submarines at dawn and even carrying bombs during the invasion scares of 1940. After the war the Tiger Moth, the last biplane trainer in the RAF, was used by eighteen University Air Squadrons and twenty-five Reserve Flying Schools until finally replaced by the Chipmunk in February 1955. British production for the RAF totalled 4668, while a further 2751 were built for the Commonwealth Air Training Plan in Australia, New Zealand and Canada.

Squadron Leader Dick Smerdon who instructed on the aircraft recalled, 'The Tiger Moth was the aircraft on which I learned to fly, was trained as a flying instructor and on which I then instructed, for a total of 500 hours. It is difficult not to become nostalgic, but the Tiger had endearing qualities. Though a simple aircraft to fly, it was not easy to fly

Below: By the outbreak of war in 1939, over 1000 de Havilland Tiger Moths had been delivered to the RAF, most of them serving with the Elementary and Reserve Flying Training Schools.

well, with ailerons on the lower mainplanes only. It was very much more comfortable to fly from the front cockpit – less slipstream, better view and in the tropics more shaded from the sun. The Tiger was such a good trainer that I had little difficulty converting to the Harvard.' Les Leetham, who went solo in 1943 wrote, 'I soloed after 11hrs dual instruction and will never forget the one thing the instructor failed to mention and could never demonstrate – the amazing difference in performance without his weight aboard. It seemed like a rocket, and at the required height for a turn, I was over the boundary instead of well upwind and this threw the whole circuit out.'

Below: The RAF's Elementary Flying Training Schools were still well stocked with Tiger Moths in the late 1940s.

POWERPLANT: One 96kW (130hp) DH Gipsy Major in-line piston engine
SPAN: 8.94m (29ft 4in); Length: 7.29m (23ft 11in)
MAX SPEED: 176km/h (109mph)
ACCOMMODATION: Tandem seating for pupil and instructor
FIRST AIRCRAFT FLOWN: 26 October 1931
ENTERED RAF SERVICE: February 1932 (Mk I - CFS)
LAST RAF SERVICE: February 1955 (UAS).

HANDLEY PAGE HEYFORD

Below: The Heyfords rotating and retractable 'dustbin' ventral turret, with Lewis gun stowed vertically, is in the lowered position of No 9 Squadron 'R' flying from RAF Scampton in the mid 1930s.

The principal obstacle to the advancement of the RAF's aircraft was the old rule, first instituted before World War I, that monoplanes were structurally dangerous and were, therefore, not to be procured for His Majesty's airmen. The Handley Page Heyford, nicknamed 'The Flying Dustbin' was the last of the RAF's biplane bombers, 124 examples being received. Throughout the 1920s, Handley Page provided the RAF with a series of excellent biplane bomber and transport aircraft, which followed from the pioneer giants of World War I. Most oddly, the Heyford's slim body was attached to the upper wing and there was a large gap between it and the thick portion of lower wing between the spatted wheels, in which were the bomb cells. It had four-blade fixed-pitch propellers and the liquid-cooled engines were in very slim nacelles.

Heyfords were generally well liked – they were pleasant to fly and popular with the crews of the eleven squadrons that were equipped with them. They were regularly flown across country in squadron formation and one of No 102 Squadron's Heyfords was looped with ease at the 1935 RAF Display at Hendon. On 26 February 1935, Dr Robert Watson-Watt used Heyford K6902 to demonstrate, in conjunction with the BBC's Daventry transmitter, the first primitive radar receiver. In his report document, Watson-Watt described not just the basic underlying principles of radar, which had never before been set forth so comprehensively, but also the

Below: No 99 Squadron became the first to equip with the Handley Page Heyford in December 1933 at RAF Upper Heyford. For their time they seemed huge, especially if you sat in the open cockpit, or in the exposed front gunners' position.

way a complete British defence system should be constructed, approximately how it would perform and how the complete system – with communications to plotting centres and fighter pilots, IFF (Identification Friend-or-Foe) would eventually function.

The reliable Heyford equipped a total of ten Bomber Command Squadrons between 1933 and

Right: Handley Page Heyford of No 9 Squadron seen in flight, March 1936. The clearance between propeller tips and fuselage was about four inches – note pilot's guard rail. The arrangement of the fuselage abutting under the surface of the top wing gave the crew a field of vision hitherto unknown in a bomber.

1939. The last front-line squadron, No 166 based at Leconfield, replaced its aircraft with Whitleys in September 1939. Three dozen or so Heyfords continued in service with the Bombing and Gunnery Schools at Aldergrove and West Freugh until August 1940.

POWERPLANT: Two 429kW (575hp) Rolls-Royce Kestrel IIIS in-line piston engines
SPAN: 22.86m (75ft 0in); **Length:** 17.68m (58ft 0in)
MAX SPEED: 230km/h (142mph)
TYPICAL ARMAMENT: Three Lewis guns in nose and midships positions and ventral 'dustbin'; Max bomb load 1209kg (2,660lb)
FIRST AIRCRAFT FLOWN: 12 June 1930
ENTERED RAF SERVICE: November 1933 (Mk I, No 99 Squadron)
LAST RAF SERVICE: April 1941 (Mk III glider tug).

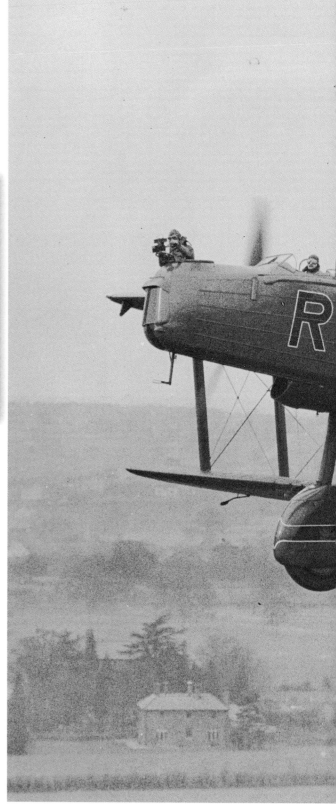

1933

AVRO ANSON

For over thirty years, wherever the RAF was based, sooner or later an example of the faithful 'Annie' would appear. Many were used to train navigators, wireless operators and air gunners. Some 400 served in Coastal Command, for whom the Anson had originally been developed, and provided the backbone until the arrival of the Lockheed Hudson. A Coastal Command Anson pilot said in 1940, 'Our chief enemy is not the German Luftwaffe or the German Navy, but boredom, which may provoke first inattention, then indifference. We spend hundreds of hours with nothing to look upon but the expanse of sea and sky – wave, on wave, on wave.' Though not very fast, it was very reliable and easy to manoeuvre and these qualities were summed up by a Coastal Command station commander, 'Anson is, as Anson does.'

The Anson was the RAF's first monoplane with a retractable undercarriage, for thousands this came to be the aircraft's most memorable feature. To raise the gear meant winding a crank lever situated under the pilot's seat, by hand, through many turns. Ian

Above: When war was declared in 1939, the Avro Anson was the mainstay of Coastal Command, serving with eleven squadrons, but they were hopelessly outdated. This is an Anson 1 of No 502 Squadron based at RAF Aldergrove for patrols off the Irish coast.

Right: The Avro Anson T20 navigation trainer featured an astrodome on top of the fuselage and a moulded plastic nose was fitted for practice bomb-aiming. The DF loop was moved back level with the fourth window.

Above: Working on the Anson's Armstrong Siddeley Cheetah engine.

McCubbery, a Wireless Operator/Air Gunner, who flew in Ansons recalled, 'My main recollection in these aircraft was of the poor trainee's job to wind up

POWERPLANT: Two 261kW (350hp) Armstrong Siddeley Cheetah IX radial piston engines (T21)
SPAN: 17.22m (56ft 6in); Length: 12.87m (42ft 3in)
MAX SPEED: 279km/h (173mph)
ACCOMMODATION: Crew of six (T21); two machine guns in side windows, 163kg (360lb) bomb load (Mk I)
FIRST AIRCRAFT FLOWN: 24 March 1935
ENTERED RAF SERVICE: 6 March 1936 (No 48 Squadron)
LAST RAF SERVICE: 28 June 1968 (C19, Southern Communications Squadron).

the undercarriage – 140-odd turns up on take off, then another 140-odd down on landing. It was a good thing we were fit and able in our early days. Once airborne, I was mainly preoccupied with the operation of the complicated 1083 Receiver/Transmitter with its odd coils kept in the boxes beside it.'

Ansons were allocated to a number of Bomber Command squadrons to give crews experience of more modern aircraft before they were rapidly converted to higher performance front-line machines. After the war, Ansons remained in use for navigational, air signalling and bombing training in a variety of marks, while Anson C19s (of which 263 were built post-World War II) were flown on light transport and communications duties until 1968.

SUPERMARINE WALRUS

The Walrus probably received more nicknames than any other type, including 'Shagbat', 'Pusser's Duck' and 'Steam Pigeon' (while being known as the Seagull V in Australia, who bought the aircraft before the RAF). It was designed for catapulting from warships and was descended from a long line of Supermarine amphibians, being adopted by the RAF after trials on the battleships HMS *Repulse* and *Variant* in 1934. All the early Walruses were delivered to the Fleet Air Arm and it was not until 1941 that the type

(subsequently built with wooden hulls by Saunders-Roe) began its career in the RAF as an air–sea rescue aircraft. Many pilots shot down in the sea owed their lives to rescue by a Walrus. Often flying near enemy coasts, risking interception and frequently alighting in mine-infested waters to effect a rescue, was heroic work which attracted little publicity.

This sturdy amphibian flew in most 1939-1945 war theatres, including the African deserts. One RAF squadron, No 277, saved 598 personnel from the 1000 aircrew who were rescued around the British

Below: A Supermarine Walrus just becoming airborne from Southampton Water in March 1936; water is dripping from its hull as it lifts off.

Above: Originally known as the Seagull V, the Supermarine Walrus served both the RAF and the Royal Navy, becoming famous as a 'maid of all work', notably in the Air–Sea Rescue role.

POWERPLANT: One 577kW (775hp) Bristol Pegasus VI radial piston engine
SPAN: 13.97m (45ft 10in); Length: 11.43m (37ft 7in)
MAX SPEED: 218km/h (135mph)
TYPICAL ARMAMENT: Up to three Vickers K guns in bows and amidships, and up to 227kg (500lb) of bombs or depth charges
FIRST AIRCRAFT FLOWN: 18 March 1936
ENTERED RAF SERVICE: 1941 (December 1941, No 277 Squadron)
LAST RAF SERVICE: April 1946 (No 269 Squadron).

Isles. At one and the same time Supermarine earned the distinction of supplying the RAF with its slowest front-line type, the Walrus, and with its fastest, the Spitfire. The Walrus caused no recognition problems as its biplane configuration, with its engine driving a pusher airscrew, and wing tip floats were very distinguishable. Its heroic work in the ASR role involved seven UK based and four Middle Eastern squadrons, while also being used for mine spotting and, on one memorable occasion, dive bombing duties!

AIRSPEED OXFORD

Above: Since they were not much used or needed the dorsal turrets were removed from Oxfords early in World War II. AT462 was a Mk 1 built by de Havilland in 1941.

The Oxford was designed from the outset as a trainer, though it had the civil Envoy as a predecessor. Fitted with a retractable undercarriage, flaps and modern equipment it was a versatile aircraft, with a removable dorsal gun turret. It was used for multi-engined pilot training, navigation, air gunnery, radio and as a bomber trainer. The Oxford's handling qualities were designed to match those of the larger multi-engine aircraft which most pupils would go on to fly. However, it was more demanding than the Anson for pilot training, and care was necessary during take-offs and landings. Robert Cooling, who trained on Oxfords with 15 SFTS at Lossiemouth recalled, 'Early take-offs, were often crescent shaped until pilots got used to the swing, but once in the air the Oxford handled well. It was responsive to the controls and generally stable.'

With a neatly streamlined fuselage, and engines mounted above the wings, the design had a pleasing appearance. The wooden frame was plywood covered, apart from the movable surfaces, which had fabric covering. Colloquially known as the 'Oxbox' or 'Oxo', it was used extensively by the Central Flying School and the expanding Flying Training Schools. Many of the Oxfords operated in Canada and Rhodesia under the Commonwealth Training

51

Above: One of the few Oxford IIs which was fitted out for ambulance duties and appropriately marked before delivery by Airspeed from its Portsmouth factory.

Below: Airspeed Oxfords of No 3 Flying Training School at RAF South Cerney in 1938. Dual controls were standard, making the Oxford suitable for use as a twin-engined pilot trainer.

POWERPLANT: Two 275kW (370hp) Armstrong Siddeley Cheetah X radial piston engines (Mk II)
SPAN: 16.25m (53ft 4in); **Length:** 10.5m (34ft 6in)
MAX SPEED: 301km/h (188mph)
TYPICAL ARMAMENT: A dorsal turret with one gun was fitted to gunnery training aircraft
FIRST AIRCRAFT FLOWN: 19 June 1937
FIRST ENTERED RAF SERVICE: November 1937 (Mk I)
LAST RAF SERVICE: 1954 (Mk II, No 10 AFTS).

Scheme, had Pratt & Whitney engines. As with other wooden aircraft of the period the casein-based adhesive used in the production caused problems, particularly in damp climates. In humid conditions, fungoid growth in the joints was common.

A total of 8586 Oxfords had been built by July 1945, some of which were also used as air ambulances, for communications, radar calibration and beam-approach training. From the end of the war they served mainly for communications duties. Squadron Leader Dick Smerdon states, 'The Oxford was distinctly British and provided the pilot with a good twin-engined trainer prior to his conversion to operational types. It introduced him to operating the [quadrant-mounted] throttles with his right hand, manipulating a 'spectacle' control column with his left hand, and flying from the left-hand seat. After the Tiger Moth and the Harvard, the view from the flight deck was much improved.'

ARMSTRONG WHITWORTH WHITLEY

In spite of being described as a 'nose down, slab-sided and plank-winged lumbering giant', the Whitley equipped frontline squadrons of Bomber Command until mid-1942 and achieved far more than was ever expected. Though it compared unfavourably with the Wellington, the Whitley had to continue into production until the Lancaster arrived in quantity. Nevertheless, the bomber that many did not want, exceeded most expectations. Its wings and fuselage gave the impression that they were travelling along different paths, but it was as steady as a rock, a docile aircraft which enjoyed the affection of its crews.

The Whitley was used from the start as a night bomber and it is particularly remembered for its early leaflet-dropping raids over Germany. It was the first RAF bomber to have a power-operated rear turret. A special version was built for anti-submarine work with Coastal Command. Together with the Hampden, it dropped the first bombs on the German mainland in May 1940 and was engaged in the first raid on Berlin in August 1940. Another field in which the Whitley later made a notable contribution was as a glider-tug and paratroop trainer with the Airborne Forces.

Below: When war was declared on 3 September 1939, six squadrons of Whitleys were ready for operations with Bomber Command's No 4 Group. Here a Whitley IV of No 10 Squadron at RAF Dishforth is being loaded with bombs for a night raid.

1937

Left: A production Armstrong Whitworth Whitley I, with Tiger VIII radial engines and a power-operated nose turret, on a test flight with No 10 Squadron. Deliveries began in the early months of 1937.

A No 10 Squadron pilot operating from RAF Dishforth leading an attack on Turin in Italy, involving a 1350-mile round trip over the Alps in June 1940 said of the raid, 'I got my heavily laden Whitley to 17,500ft over the Alps flying blind on my instruments. We knew we were crossing them because of the bumps which the aircraft felt every time it crossed a peak. On we went until I judged we were in the murk over Turin. Then I let go a flare which lit up the middle of the city. I ran in at 5000ft, dropped two bombs, one of which burst on the Fiat building, the other in the railway sidings beside it. The Italian gunners were detonating their shells about a mile above our heads expecting us to be flying at 10,000ft.'

Above: The Armstrong Whitworth Whitley, chosen by the RAF in August 1935 to re-equip the heavy bomber squadrons. It continued in that role until the spring of 1942, later seeing service with Coastal Command. This is a Whitley V of No 78 Squadron.

POWERPLANT: Two 853kW (1145hp) Rolls-Royce Merlin X in-line piston engine (Mk V)
SPAN: 25.6m (84ft 0in); Length: 21.5m (70ft 6in)
MAX SPEED: 357km/h (222mph)
TYPICAL ARMAMENT: Four 0.303in guns in tail turret and one in nose turret; Max bomb load 3181kg (7000lb)
FIRST AIRCRAFT FLOWN: 4 June 1935
ENTERED RAF SERVICE: March 1937 (Mk I, No 10 Squadron)
LAST RAF SERVICE: 1943 (Mk V, No 21 HGCU).

BRISTOL BLENHEIM

Below A Blenheim IV of No 110 Squadron being refuelled and loaded with 250lb GP bombs and SBCs at RAF Wattisham in 1940. The 'long-nosed' Mk IV version was the RAF's most numerous operational aircraft during the first year of hostilities.

In 1934 Viscount Rothermere instructed the Bristol Aeroplane Company to build him a passenger aircraft that would be 'the best in the world'. Within a year, the Britain First was delivered and he immediately donated it to the RAF. This Bristol Type 142 became the prototype for the Blenheim, which was faster than most fighters then in service.

Although the Blenheim was a very advanced light bomber for the mid-1930s and comparable with other new aircraft being developed in Germany and elsewhere, by the outbreak of World War II it was obsolete. In the Battle of France in 1940, Blenheim Is suffered crippling losses, being no match for Luftwaffe fighters. Blenheims then served in Coastal Command, in the Middle East and in Malaya. Some were converted into fighters and were fitted with a battery of four Browning machine guns under the fuselage. The first-ever radar interception by a night fighter was achieved by a Blenheim IF.

Richard Passmore, a Blenheim air gunner wrote, 'In the early days of the war, Blenheims were sent over the Channel on solo raids, and usually in daylight. It was my duty to fend off any attacking fighters from my turret on top of the fuselage. I did this in the knowledge that the range of my gun was inadequate, and that it was me who was most likely to be killed. So the pilots invariably tried to stay out of

Left: A Bristol Blenheim IV of No 139 (Bomber) Squadron based at RAF Horsham St Faith in 1940. The Blenheim-equipped daylight bombing squadrons suffered major losses during the early stages of World War II.

sight in cloud. But invariably the cloud rolled back a few miles north of the French coast, leaving a beautifully dangerous blue sky.'

The long-nosed Blenheim IV had a stepped windscreen and a twin-gun turret, and became the first RAF aircraft to cross the German border on 3 September 1939. Aircraft of Nos 107 and 110 Squadrons from Wattisham also participated in the very first raid of World War II, attacking part of the German fleet. No 2 Group Blenheims bore the brunt of daylight operations over Europe in 1940 and 1941, but suffered heavy casualties.

POWERPLANT: Two 686kW (920hp) Bristol Mercury XV radial piston engine (Mark IV)
SPAN: 17.17m (56ft 4in); Length: 13.00m (42ft 9in)
MAX SPEED: 428km/h (266mph)
TYPICAL ARMAMENT: One fixed 0.303in Browning gun in port wing; twin guns, remotely aimed and fired, in Frazer Nash undernose mounting firing aft, and twin 0.303 guns in dorsal turret; Max bomb load 600 kg (1320lb)
FIRST AIRCRAFT FLOWN: 25 June 1936
ENTERED RAF SERVICE: 10 March 1937 (Mk I, No 114 Squadron)
LAST RAF SERVICE: April 1944 (Mk V, No 244 Squadron).

Above: Bristol Blenheim Is were used in the 1940–41 Middle East campaigns and during the fight for Greece. This is a No 11 Squadron example.

FAIREY BATTLE

Right: The Fairey Battle is remembered as a combat aircraft which seemed marvellous at the time when it appeared and yet which, within four years, was being hacked out of the sky by the Luftwaffe and anti-aircraft guns on the ground.

Below: Fairey Battles of No 218 Squadron suffered heavy losses in France. Survivors like K9324 (**centre**) were placed mostly overseas into the Empire Training Scheme. The other two depicted were shot down on 12 May 1940.

Unfortunately, various factors conspired to make the elegant Battle, with its rugged advanced construction and retractable undercarriage, a somewhat unsuccessful product of the pre-World War II 'Expansion Scheme'. One historian described it, 'As well adapted for air fighting as hackneys for winning the Derby!' Designed as a replacement for the biplane day bomber, Fairey wanted to use the new 24-cylinder Prince 'double' engine driving contra-rotating propellers, but had to settle for the Rolls-Royce Merlin, which left it underpowered for its task.

Development of larger bomber types lagged so badly behind that Battles were produced in substantial numbers (a total of 2196), when they were already outmoded. No other type of British bomber suffered so harshly at the hands of the enemy in such a short time – in five-weeks in mid-1940, 115 were lost on operations. The Battle was already dangerously out of date two years before it was called upon to support the British Expeditionary Force in France.

Above: There was nothing that the pilots of RAF Fairey Battles could do – it was simply a sitting duck for the Luftwaffe's fighters.

POWERPLANT: One 768kW (1030hp) Rolls-Royce Merlin I, II, III or V in-line piston engine
SPAN: 16.46m (54ft 0in); Length: 12.85m (42ft 1.75in)
MAX SPEED: 388km/h (241mph)
TYPICAL ARMAMENT: One 0.303in Browning machine gun forward and one Vickers gun aft; Max bomb load 454kg (1000lb)
FIRST AIRCRAFT FLOWN: 10 March 1936
ENTERED RAF SERVICE: May 1937 (Mk I, No 63 Squadron)
LAST RAF SERVICE: July 1944 (TTI).

The attack on the Meuse bridge at Maastricht on 12 May 1940 by five Battles of No 12 Squadron, when Flight Officer D E Garland and Sergeant T Gray were posthumously awarded the VC, is now legendary. Another Battle pilot, who flew later in the same day, reported, 'The situation continued to deteriorate and by 2.00 pm a much larger force was standing by to attack this and four other bridges between Mouzon and Sedan. Sixty-seven Battles took off soon after 3.00 pm. Thirty-two returned. The rest had fallen victims to intense AA fire and to the German fighters, which were so numerous that they could not all be driven away. Two pontoon bridges were destroyed, another damaged, and two permanent bridges received direct hits. The bridges were broken; so were the French!'

GLOSTER GLADIATOR

The Gladiator's years of service marked the end of an era in the RAF which began with the RFC biplanes of 1911 – it was the service's last biplane fighter, being built to fill the interlude before the new monoplane types would be available in quantity. It was a direct descendant and an aerodynamic refinement of its predecessor, the Gauntlet and featured an enclosed cockpit. Gladiators formed the only defence of Malta, when Italy entered the war, and No 261 Squadron's three aircraft named *Faith*, *Hope* and *Charity* were famous survivors.

During the Battle of Britain some were used as night fighters for the defence of Plymouth. In the same year, 1940, they also distinguished themselves while operating from a frozen lake during the Norwegian campaign. Gladiators also equipped the early wartime Meteorological Flights. They would climb to height, recording temperatures and humidity, providing valuable information to the Met Office to form the basis of weather forecasts upon

Above right: Gloster Gladiator in the colours of No 239 Squadron in 1940. This example, built in 1937 at Hucclecote, Gloucester was purchased by Glosters in 1948 and subsequently rebuilt to flying condition. It was presented to the Shuttleworth Trust on 7 November 1960 and remains airworthy at Old Warden.

Right: As a concession to modern design, the Gloster Gladiator featured a sliding canopy for the pilot, although most RAF pilots said at the time that they still preferred the wind in their faces.

which planning for operational missions was based. Apart from service in the Western Desert, Gladiators also equipped the British Expeditionary Force which went to the assistance of Greece when that country was invaded by Italy.

Flight Lieutenant W J Woods described an early combat mission in Malta, 'During the day there were constant raids. The Italian bombers continued to fly over at high altitudes, in faultless formation and the accuracy of their high-level bombing earned grudging respect. Our Gladiators, *Faith*, *Hope* and *Charity* took off from Hal Far to fight greatly superior numbers. People in the streets cheered us and our photographs appeared in shop windows, but we were only three against all the Regia Aeronautica in Sicily. I sighted a formation of five S.79 enemy aircraft approaching Valetta at 15,000ft. I delivered an attack from the astern, and got a good burst at a range of approximately 200 yds. He went down in a steep dive with black smoke pouring from his tail! I could not follow him down, but he appeared to go into the sea. I then broke away and returned over the island at 11,000ft south of Grand Harbour.'

POWERPLANT: One 626kW (840hp) Bristol Mercury IX radial piston engine
SPAN: 9.85m (32ft 3in); Length: 8.38m (27ft 5in)
MAX SPEED: 407km/h (253mph)
TYPICAL ARMAMENT: Four 0.303in Browning machine guns, two in the fuselage and two below the lower wings
FIRST AIRCRAFT FLOWN: 12 September 1934
ENTERED RAF SERVICE: February 1937 (No 72 Squadron)
LAST RAF SERVICE: January 1942 (No 6 Squadron).

Right: The Gladiator was in effect a single-bay adaptation of the Gloster Gauntlet with flaps on upper and lower wings and single-leg cantilever landing gear.

HAWKER HURRICANE

Hawker Aircraft was convinced that only a monoplane could significantly improve fighter performance in the late 1930s. Designer, Sydney Camm persuaded the Air Ministry that the private venture Hurricane was a worthy type for official sponsorship and obtained an order for a prototype. With a retractable undercarriage, flaps and an enclosed cockpit, it had many novel features for that era. Rolls-Royce had a new 1000hp aero engine under development and a 300mph monoplane became an obvious possibility. The Air Ministry insisted on eight-gun firepower, but in the mid-1930s only rifle-calibre armament was available.

The prototype first flew on 6 November 1935 in the hands of Chief Test Pilot 'George' Bulman. On landing after the maiden flight, Bulman told Camm, 'It is a piece of cake, I could even teach you to fly her in half-an-hour.' Following service entry with No 111 Squadron at Northolt in 1937, squadron re-equipment was rapid and at the outbreak of World War II, sixteen front-line RAF fighter squadrons had Hurricane Is on strength. The type was at the forefront of the 1939–40 air war over France, but it was in the Battle of Britain that it really won its spurs. Hurricane pilots shot down the greatest number of enemy aircraft, accounting for more than the total destroyed by all other defences combined.

The 1940 victories confirmed that Camm's design had qualities which compensated for lack of performance, and this view was further confirmed

Below and right: A Canadian manufactured Hawker Hurricane XII, painted in No 71 'Eagle' Squadron markings. It remains airworthy with The Fighter Collection, based at the Imperial War Museum at Duxford.

during operations overseas. Modification of a number of Hurricanes to fighter–bomber status (popularly known as 'Hurribombers') saw these aircraft operate with distinction in both Europe and the Western Desert – as more Spitfires entered service closer to home (though night fighter Hurricanes continued intruder sorties), work in the latter theatre continued the success story of the Hawker machine in the ground attack role, using rockets and 40mm guns with which the aircraft's sturdy construction could cope.

Wing Commander Bob Stanford-Tuck, who commanded No 257 Squadron with Hurricanes during the Battle of Britain, summed it up thus, 'My reaction to my first flight in the Hurricane after the Spitfire was not good. She seemed like a flying brick, a great lumbering stallion. But, after the first few minutes I found the Hurricane's virtues. She was solid. She was as steady as a rock and was a wonderful gun platform. Somehow she gave the pilot terrific confidence. You felt entirely safe in this plane.'

POWERPLANT: One 768kW (1030hp) Rolls-Royce Merlin II or III in-line piston engine (Mk I)
SPAN: 12.19m (40ft 0in); Length; 9.75m (32ft 0in)
MAX SPEED: 511km/h (318mph)
TYPICAL ARMAMENT: Eight 0.303 Browning guns (Mk I)
FIRST AIRCRAFT FLOWN: 6 November 1935
ENTERED RAF SERVICE: December 1937 (Mk I, No 111 Squadron)
LAST RAF SERVICE: January 1947 (Mk IV, No 6 Squadron).

Left : Echelon formation of Hawker Hurricane IICs of No 1 Squadron airborne from RAF Acklington in September 1942, a sortie prior to the squadron converting to Typhoons.

Below: Hurricane IICs also operated as fighter-bombers and continued their offensive operations well into 1942. Five squadrons participated in the historic Dieppe raid on 19 August 1942.

HANDLEY PAGE HAMPDEN

W hen it first appeared the Hampden, nicknamed the 'Flying Panhandle' and 'Flying Tadpole', marked a considerable improvement over existing RAF bomber designs. Very experienced in the manufacture of heavy bombers, Handley Page had finally rejected the biplane in favour of all-metal monoplane construction. Unfortunately, the Hampden for all its bold unorthodoxy had 'built-in' obsolescence! Its unusual fuselage construction and general layout left no room – literally – for further development. But it served as a stop-gap for the first two years of war operations. Although the Hampden's operational exploits were overshadowed by those of its larger successor and stablemate, the Halifax, it was one of the quartet of British twin-engined bombers which embarked on the RAF's bombing offensive. Ten squadrons equipped with Hampdens were almost continuously in action over the continent during the first two years of the war.

The excellent manoeuvrability of the Hampden was recorded by Flight Officer Guy Gibson (later Wing Commander Guy Gibson, VC, DSO, DFC) of No 83 Squadron in August 1940, 'Flying L4070, returning from a raid over Lorient, I spotted a Dornier Do215 below me and I used the Hampden as a "fighter–bomber" diving down to shoot him down with my fixed gun.'

Above: Modified bomb doors and additional guns were featured on the Handley Page Hampden TBR1 torpedo strike version shown here in the hands of the Torpedo Development Unit, Gosport in 1942.

POWERPLANT: Two 746kW (1000hp) Bristol Pegasus XVIII radial piston engines
SPAN: 21.98m (69ft 2in); Length: 16.33m (53ft 7in)
MAX SPEED: 410km/h (254mph)
TYPICAL ARMAMENT: One fixed and one portable 0.303in gun forward and twin 0.303in guns in dorsal and ventral positions; Max bomb load 1818kg (4,000lb)
FIRST AIRCRAFT FLOWN: 21 June 1936
ENTERED RAF SERVICE: August 1938 (Mk I, No 49 Squadron)
LAST RAF SERVICE: December 1943 (TBI, Nos 455 and 489 Squadrons).

Sergeant John Hannah, an 18-year-old Wireless Operator/Air Gunner with No 83 Squadron, flew Hampden P1355 from Scampton on 15 September 1940 for a raid on Antwerp. He reported to the pilot on the intercom, 'The bombs are away, but an incendiary shell has exploded in the bomb bay, a hail of shrapnel has ripped through the mid-wing section and pierced the wing fuel tanks. The aircraft is on fire... I am going out in the slipstream onto the wing with a fire extinguisher and use my parachute pack to extinguish the flames... The fire is out, Sir.' On landing, John Hannah was taken straight to hospital for treatment to extensive burns — and later came the official announcement of the award of a Victoria Cross.

NORTH AMERICA
HARVARD

Above: Harvard Is, like these of No 2 Special Flying Training School at Brize Norton were introduced to RAF service before the outbreak of World War II. This SFTS was formed with an establishment of 31 Harvards.

The Harvard, first delivered to the RAF in December 1938 with No 12 FTS at Grantham, remained standard equipment at Flying Training Schools for over sixteen years, until being finally superseded by Vampire T11s. With the outbreak of World War II on the horizon, the RAF realized that home aircraft production would be concentrated on operational types and unlikely to be able to meet training aircraft requirements.

Therefore, a stop-gap order was issued for 400 North American BC-1s, named Harvard I for RAF service, which was already flying with the US Army Air Corps. Eventually 4765 were delivered, including a number built in Canada, the bulk going to the overseas flying schools in Canada, Rhodesia and South Africa.

The Harvard's characteristic rasping note – caused by its direct-drive propeller with high tip

speeds – was a familiar sound near any training airfield until the mid-50s. The trainer is long remembered by the thousands of instructors and students who flew it, with some affection, although there was criticism, mainly regarding visibility from the cockpit. The view forward from either seat was poor, a severe handicap for a training aircraft, especially for taxiing, take-off and landing. The Harvard was a strong aircraft but it could bite the unwary student if it was not properly handled. It could flick suddenly without warning, and landings could cause problems if the tail was held too high, although pupils were taught not to throttle back until the main wheels were on the ground. The Harvard was also prone to ground-looping.

Squadron Leader Dick Smerdon recalled his Harvard days whilst in Egypt, 'This was my first introduction to brakes, a constant-speed propeller and an American radial engine. The use of these items gave me a lasting preference for hydraulic brakes in contrast to the British pneumatics, and an admiration for the trouble-free radial engine – no overheating, even in the tropics.' Another instructor said, 'I enjoyed flying the Harvard. I don't remember many

vices, except that if you relaxed after landing, it would quickly ground-loop on you. When you think about it, spinning is the worst that can happen to you, and it does give you confidence to know you can cope.'

POWERPLANT: One 410kW (550hp) Pratt & Whitney Wasp R-1340-49 radial engine
SPAN: 13.05m (42ft 10in); Length: 8.83m (29ft 0in)
MAX SPEED: 330km/h (205mph)
ACCOMMODATION: Two seats in tandem
FIRST AIRCRAFT FLOWN: 1937
ENTERED RAF SERVICE: December 1938 (Mk I)
LAST RAF SERVICE: 1955 (Mk IIB, No 3 FTS).

Below: The NA Harvard saw long service with the RAF, but none longer than this aircraft that has been used by the A&AEE at Boscombe Down for over fifty years as a photographic/low speed chase aircraft.

Right: The Harvard was one of the first US aircraft ordered by the British Purchasing Commission for the RAF in June 1938. An initial batch of 200 was delivered by September 1939.

SHORT SUNDERLAND

Above: A Short Sunderland I of No 10 Squadron at RAF Mount Batten, Plymouth on patrol over the Western Approaches in 1941, showing the two dorsal gunners turrets fitted early in the war.

Right: A Sunderland V of No 201 Squadron after landing on Havel Lake on 16 September 1948, during the Berlin Airlift, with its contents being loaded onto barges. The tonnage carried by the flying boats was relatively small but the Berliners were impressed with their contribution.

The Sunderland, built by Short Bros alongside the similar, civilian, Empire flying boats, first entered service with the RAF in 1938. At the outbreak of World War II four RAF squadrons were equipped with Sunderlands, the only long distance aircraft available to Coastal Command.

'The Battle of the Atlantic was the dominating factor all through the war', wrote Sir Winston Churchill – and it was in that battle against enemy U-boats that the Sunderland, with its twelve hours duration, may be best remembered. The first U-boat kill came in January 1940, and by mid-1942 new depth charges coming into service with Coastal Command, provided Sunderland crews with a more effective weapon against submarines.

Flight Officer E R Baker, skipper of a Sunderland of No 210 Squadron based at Pembroke Dock, South Wales, recalled a convoy protection sortie on 16 August 1940, 'We were concerned about the atrocious weather conditions with driving rain and a cloud base hardly higher than 400ft. Six hours later the weather had hardly improved when the second pilot shouted, "Sub" and I immediately sounded the Klaxon. The crew jumped to their action stations. The U-boat was on the surface but started a crash dive when it saw us. I was diving low over it to drop a depth charge. The whole surface of the sea seemed to

Above: The Sunderland's high-wing allowed the four radial engines and propellers to be reasonably clear of spray, and the fixed wing-tip floats provided stability on the water.

shudder for yards around and then suddenly blew up! In the middle of the boiling sea the submarine emerged with its decks awash, and then sank rather like a brick. Then great globs of oil began to spread. I signalled a destroyer and circled for an hour.' Baker received a DFC for the attack. His victim, U-51, was in fact seriously damaged, but not sunk.

The Twin Wasp-powered Sunderland V continued in use after the war, notching up impressive sortie totals in the transport role during the Korean War, the Berlin Airlift (operating from the city's lakes) and the 1951–54 Greenland Expedition.

POWERPLANT: Four 895kW (1,200hp) Pratt & Whitney Twin Wasp R-1830 radial piston engines (Mk V)
Span: 34.37m (112ft 9.5in); Length: 26.00m (85ft 4in)
MAX SPEED: 344km/h (213mph)
TYPICAL ARMAMENT: Two 0.303in guns in nose turret and four in tail turret, plus two manually-operated 0.50in beam guns; Max bomb load 909kg (2000lb)
FIRST AIRCRAFT FLOWN: 16 October 1937
ENTERED RAF SERVICE: June 1938 (Mk I, Nos 210 and 230 Squadrons)
LAST RAF SERVICE: 15 May 1959 (MR5, No 205 Squadron).

SUPERMARINE SPITFIRE

The progressive thinking of aircraft designer R J Mitchell at Supermarine, produced the Spitfire, the most famous RAF fighter of World War II. Through work for the RAF's High Speed Flight and its Schneider Trophy contenders, that culminated in outright victory for Britain in 1931, the company knew more than anyone about streamlining, structural stressing, control surface flutter and other special problems associated with high-speed flight. After the successful first flight of the prototype in 1936 an order for 310 aircraft was placed and the name Spitfire chosen. 'Just the sort of bloody silly name they would choose', commented Reginald Mitchell.

Production of Spitfire Is commenced in 1937, the first service examples going to No 19 Squadron at Duxford a year later. Nine units were operational when war broke out, ten more having been added to Fighter Command's strength by the start of the Battle of Britain. External armour-glass windscreens were provided at the insistence of Fighter Command's Commander-in-Chief ACM Hugh 'Stuffy' Dowding, who pointed out that, 'If Chicago gangsters could ride behind bullet-proof glass, he saw no reason why his pilots should not.' Dowding insisted that 'his' Spitfire squadrons were not sent to France but kept for home defence, 957 being the average strength over the summer of 1940 (albeit some 400 less than there were Hurricanes).

Successive marks of Merlin-engined Spitfire saw many refinements and more major changes to Mitchell's design, primarily concerned with the armament and powerplant. The Spitfire V powered by the RR Merlin 45 engine was the first to see action

Below: From 1944 onwards 1054 Spitfire XVIs were delivered, the type going into service with the RAF 2nd TAF as a ground-attack aircraft. This aircraft has a tear-drop cockpit, clipped wings and an enlarged rudder.

1938

Left: Now owned and operated by The Shuttleworth Collection, this clipped-wing Spitfire VC was the first mark to carry cannon armament.

Above: Spitfires were supplied immediately before the war to a number of Auxiliary Air Force squadrons. These are with No 609 (West Riding) Squadron at RAF Catterick in August 1939.

POWERPLANT: One 1073.8kW (1440hp) Rolls-Royce Merlin 45 V-12 in-line piston engine (Mk V)
SPAN: 11.23m (36ft 10in); clipped wing 9.93m (32ft 7in);
LENGTH: 9.12m (29ft 11in)
MAX SPEED: 603km/h (374mph)
Typical armament: Two 20mm and four 0.303 Browning machine guns, or four 20mm guns and one 227kg (500lb) bomb (LFVC)
FIRST AIRCRAFT FLOWN: 5 March 1936
ENTERED RAF SERVICE: 29 July 1938 (Mk I, No 19 Squadron)
LAST RAF SERVICE: June 1957 (PR19, THUM Flight, Woodvale).

as a fighter–bomber, and was well used overseas, particularly in the Western Desert and the Far East. The next major change came in 1942 with the Spitfire IX, improved performance, especially at high altitude, coming from the Merlin 61 engine. This powerplant was also used in the Spitfire VIII, which flew primarily in the Far East and Italy and the PRXI photo-reconnaissance derivative. Spitfire XVIs had Packard-built Merlins and mainly flew in the fighter–bomber role. These and Mk IXs made up a large part of the Second Tactical Air Force (2TAF) in Europe at the time of D-Day.

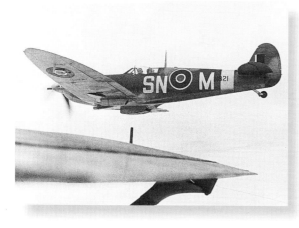

Left: The more powerful Merlin 45 engine, elliptical wings, and revised armament are evident in this Spitfire Vb of No 243 Squadron at RAF Ouston in June 1942.

Introduction of the RR Griffon engine saw, by the end of production, a doubling in power compared with the original Spitfire I. The first major variant with the new powerplant was the Spitfire XIV, used successfully by home units against V1 flying bombs and in Europe with 2TAF. Post-war, the Mk XVIII continued the improvements, seeing action with Far East-based squadrons in Malaya, while the PRXIX was the last of the photo-recce marks, and was the last Spitfire version to serve with the RAF. The final production variants, the F21 of 1944 no longer had elliptical wings; the F22 had a cut-down rear fuselage with a bubble canopy, and the further developed F24 ended Spitfire production in 1948. The Spitfire will always be regarded as a classic example of British aeronautical achievement.

Right: One of the RAF Battle of Britain Memorial Flight's Spitfires, this Mk IIa was built at the Castle Bromwich 'Shadow Factory' in August 1940 and was just too late to take part in the Battle of Britain.

Below: Soon after D-Day Spitfire IXs moved to Advanced Landing Grounds (ALGs) in Normandy from where No 403 Squadron, one of whose Spitfires is seen here, was one of the high scorers. Note the broken wooden propeller blades.

1938

VICKERS WELLINGTON

esigned by Barnes Wallis, the Wellington twin-engined bomber, first entered service with No 99 Squadron at RAF Mildenhall in October 1938. Known as the 'Wimpy', the ingenious geodetic structure gave the bomber such inherent strength and resilience that it could keep on flying when other aircraft would have found it all but impossible because of the damage sustained. The

Wellington bore the brunt of early wartime operations over Germany by Bomber Command, before its new four-engined machines came into service – aircraft of Nos 9 and 149 Squadrons attacked German ships on the second day of hostilities.

These early daylight raids were soon curtailed. It had been misguidedly believed that bombers required no fighter escort on daylight missions, as the

Below: A Vickers Wellington III of No 9 Squadron, with a Spitfire alongside. Vickers produced the best bomber available to the RAF at the beginning of World War II.

Above: Bristol Hercules engines gave the Wellington X a much improved performance, particularly with a full bomb load. It was the most efficient and numerous of all Wellingtons.

combined fire of the bomber formation supposedly afforded sufficient protection against interceptors. The Wellington was switched to night bombing and made the first raid on Berlin, in August 1940. It continued to participate in strength in Bomber Command's night missions until October 1943.

Squadron Leader Fred 'Popeye' Lucas, a flight commander of No 75 (NZ) Squadron said of the Wellington, 'It was a wonderful plane to handle. It did have its little characteristics which made it rather eccentric, such as the change of trim that resulted from extending the flaps. Getting into the Wellington's cockpit was an experience in itself, for access was through a shin-barking trap-door under the nose, calling for some athletic ability.'

A pilot involved in making the film *The Lion has Wings* in 1940 reported, 'Some memories of the Wimpy are of discomfort and endurance. For example, in winter the normally cold bomber would grow colder still. Ice would build up on the propeller

Above: A typical scene on a wartime Bomber Command station; a Wellington 1C of No 149 Squadron bombing up at RAF Mildenhall in 1941.

POWERPLANT:
Two 745kW (1000hp) Bristol Pegasus XVIII radial engines (Mk IC)
SPAN: 26.26m (86ft 2in); Length: 19.86m (64ft 7in)
MAX SPEED: 379km/h (235mph)
TYPICAL ARMAMENT: Max bomb load 2045kg (4,500lb); two 0.303in guns in each of nose and tail turrets, and two manually-operated 0.303in guns in beam positions
FIRST AIRCRAFT FLOWN: 15 June 1936
ENTERED RAF SERVICE: October 1938 (Mk IC, No 99 Squadron)
LAST RAF SERVICE: 1953 (T10, No 201 AFS).

blades and fly off in chunks, slicing straight through the fabric at either side, just about level with the cockpit. The freezing gale that tore through the holes would mean that the pilot and co-pilot would have to be lifted bodily from their seats at the end of a trip and man-handled out of the aircraft, scarcely able to move.'

WESTLAND LYSANDER

Above: Although it could land on a football pitch and snatch a message with its belly-mounted hook, the Westland Lysander was too large for close support work with the Army.

When the design of the Lysander was started, the advice of the 'customers', the Army Co-operation pilots, was sought. The resulting aircraft was able to perform all of the specified tasks. It was the first fully slotted and flapped aircraft to go into RAF service, features that enabled it to land and take-off in the length of a football pitch with astonishing ease.

Westland's Chief Test Pilot, Harald Penrose reported after its maiden flight at Boscombe Down, 'On 15 June 1936, less than a year since inception of design, P8 [as it was then known] was ready for flight. There were the usual preliminary "straights" and inspections – then heading in a westerly breeze she took off in less than 150 yds and climbed away. Stalls showed the full virtue of slots except for a change of trim on opening. Controls were a little heavy but could be later adjusted with servo-tabs. When it came

to landing, I ran out of elevator when ten feet up because the tailplane was not adjustable, so the engine had to be used to help flatten out. There was a tentative round of applause while I taxied in – at least there's nothing to prevent flying back to Yeovil right away, I told Teddy' [Teddy Petter, Westland Chief Designer].

Lysander operations in World War II commenced with artillery spotting and reconnaissance. No 4 Squadron's aircraft were the last of the British Expeditionary Force Air Component to leave France in 1940 following their last minute work in dropping supplies to troops and attacking German emplacements. The Lysander's particular claim to fame was the clandestine 'spy running' night operations into occupied France. Some sixty-two missions were flown before the Allied landings, enabling over a hundred agents to be dropped off in

1938

Left: V9281 is a Canadian-built Westland Lysander IIIA that is currently airworthy in the UK. During the Dunkirk evacuation in May and June 1940, Lysanders dropped supplies to troops defending Calais and made many attacks on German positions.

Below: The Lysander II was the standard army co-operation aircraft used by the RAF in the Air Component of the BEF in France in 1940.

hostile territory.

A member of the Special Operations Executive wrote about flying the Lysander, 'The wings were fitted with automatic slats which lifted away from the leading edge as the speed decreased towards the minimum. Slow speed flight was, therefore, greatly simplified and it was possible to bring a Lysander down to land, if not like a lift, at least like an escalator.'

POWERPLANT: One 648kW (870hp) Bristol Mercury XX or XXX radial piston engine (Mk III)
SPAN: 15.24m (50ft 0in); Length; 9.29m (30ft 6in)
MAX SPEED: 306km/h (190mph)
TYPICAL ARMAMENT: Twin 0.303in Browning in rear cockpit; Max bomb load of up to two 114kg (250lb) on stub wings
FIRST AIRCRAFT FLOWN: 15 June 1936
ENTERED RAF SERVICE: May 1938 (Mk I, No 16 Squadron)
LAST RAF SERVICE: November 1945 (Mk III SD, No 357 Squadron).

WORLD WAR II

BOULTON PAUL DEFIANT

The Defiant was introduced to replace the Hawker Demon in Fighter Command, but there were conflicting views as to whether the two-seat interceptor had any real place at all in the fighter inventory. It was later said of Boulton Paul's design, 'Had it shed its turret, acquired wing guns and an AI operator instead of a gunner, what a useful aeroplane it could have become!' Control of the Defiant was vested in the gunner, making it essential that the pair operated as a team – none too easy for a fighter pilot. Operationally, the Defiant was a disappointment since its design took no account of fighter-escorted bombers flying higher than expected.

An RAF Farnborough pilot reported in May 1940, 'Compared with the Hurricane, the Defiant is heavier and has a smaller wing, so is a poor performer in combat. Its one asset is that the gunner can drive his guns quickly on target with a control stick and may achieve successes due to the Luftwaffe thinking they are Hurricanes.'

The first effective night fighter radar was the British AI Mk IV that was fitted to the Defiant. It was flown with some success in this role, but the radar-equipped version proved too slow and again suffered from lack of forward-firing guns. A night fighter pilot later recorded, 'During the night Blitz of 1940-41 the Defiant shot down more enemy aircraft than any other type, and had more kills per interception and more interceptions per hundred sorties... Curiously, nothing was done to develop either the NF Defiant itself or the valuable attribute of upward-firing armament.'

POWERPLANT: One 939kW (1260hp) Rolls-Royce Merlin XX in-line piston engine (Mk II)
SPAN: 12.0m (39ft 4in); **Length:** 10.75m (35ft 4in)
MAX SPEED: 508km/h (315mph)
TYPICAL ARMAMENT: Four 0.303in machine guns in power-operated turret amidships
FIRST AIRCRAFT FLOWN
11 August 1937
ENTERED RAF SERVICE: December 1939 (Mk I, No 264 Squadron)
LAST RAF SERVICE: April 1945 (TTIII).

Left: After leaving squadrons, Defiants continued in support roles including as target-tugs. Here a TT III is seen with a wind-operated winch on the starboard side.

Above: Boulton Paul Defiant II
night fighter of No 256 Squadron
at RAF Squires Gate, Blackpool
with turret fairings retracted, in
October 1941.

BRISTOL BEAUFORT

Opposite page: The Bristol Beaufort was designed specifically as a torpedo bomber. Developing the techniques and acquiring the skill needed to drop a torpedo accurately was undertaken at TDU Gosport and the TTUs.

Below: From 1 August 1942, Beauforts were retired from Coastal Command operations and moved to Malta, Egypt and Ceylon. This Beaufort is operating from a Western Desert strip.

The Beaufort was derived from the Blenheim, and, being a torpedo bomber, the Air Ministry stipulated a crew of four, so the aircraft was inevitably heavier. The new Bristol Taurus engine had to be used and this had early teething troubles, but two Coastal Command squadrons were operational with the Beaufort by August 1940.

Torpedo attacks on enemy shipping were the primary role of Coastal Command Beauforts, but they also assisted Blenheims in low-flying attacks with bombs and mines on barge concentrations in the ports of Northern France, Holland and Belgium. They were employed in attacks on the German battleships *Scharnhorst* and *Gneisenau* at Brest.

The Germans were forced to provide greatly strengthened defences for their coastal shipping, both by the use of flak ships and of fighters. But in this new combat environment the Beaufort lacked adequate speed and manoeuvrability to penetrate such defences successfully, and the introduction of the torpedo-carrying Beaufighter signalled its demise. On 6 April 1941, Flight Officer Ken Campbell took off from RAF St Eval on his twentieth operational sortie in Beaufort N1016 of No 22 Squadron for a daylight attack on Brest. Campbell made his attack on the German battleships at about 300ft across the outer harbour, then dropped to 50ft as the inner harbour's stone wall came into view. With less than 500yds between this mole and his target, Campbell roared between the masts of several protecting flak ships, released his torpedo and started to climb away,

Above: Early Beauforts had Bristol Taurus engines which were often troublesome. This Beaufort II had more powerful and more reliable Pratt & Whitney Twin Wasps featured by this Beaufort of No 86 Squadron based at Thorney Island.

heading for the only cover available behind the hills surrounding Brest. At that moment, the German defences opened up, a withering wall of fire focused on the Beaufort and it crashed in the harbour. The torpedo had struck the *Gneisenau*, forcing the Germans to rush it into dry dock for eight months. Campbell was awarded a posthumous VC.

The final strike by Beauforts from bases in Britain was flown in May 1942, when No 42 Squadron attacked the *Prinz Eugen* in the North Sea, sadly losing seven aircraft, despite anti-flak support by escorting Beaufighters. Beauforts also served in Malta, Egypt and Ceylon.

POWERPLANT: Two 843kW (1130hp) Bristol Taurus XII radial piston engines (Mk II)
SPAN: 17.63m (57ft 10in); Length: 13.46m (44ft 2in)
MAX SPEED: 418km/h (260mph)
TYPICAL ARMAMENT: Two 0.303in Vickers K in dorsal turret, one fixed forward-firing gun in left wing and one 0.303in Browning in remote-control chin blister; one 18in torpedo or bomb load of 907kg (2000lb)
FIRST AIRCRAFT FLOWN: 15 October 1938
ENTERED RAF SERVICE: November 1939 (Mk I, No 22 Squadron)
LAST RAF SERVICE: 10 September 1944 (Mk II, No 217 Sqn); December 1946 (Mk IIA, No 17 SFTS, Spittlegate).

LOCKHEED HUDSON

In April 1938, a UK purchasing commission was set up to explore the possibility of US aircraft fulfilling tasks that the British aircraft industry was having difficulty in meeting. A reconnaissance bomber to supplement Coastal Command's Ansons was needed for North Sea operations and a military variant of the Lockheed Model 14 airliner was investigated and chosen.

With the outbreak of war, Hudsons were amongst the first RAF aircraft to begin operations. Much action was subsequently seen off Norway, and over the Channel during the Dunkirk evacuations in addition to patrol work over the Western Approaches, Iceland and the North Sea. From 1939 until 1944 the Hudson was the standard Coastal Command landplane, and was used by many squadrons. Following Dunkirk, two squadrons moved to Northern Ireland to strengthen the anti-U-boat forces and some took part in the hunt for the Bismarck in April 1941. During 1941–42, Hudsons were especially active off the Norwegian coast and the Hook of Holland, attacking enemy shipping. Whilst on anti-shipping patrols, between August 1941 and October 1943, they were involved in the destruction or surrender of no fewer than twenty-four U-boats.

Perhaps the best known search that was carried out was to find the German prison ship *Altmark*, which had many captured British seamen on board. A Hudson pilot recalled, 'The *Altmark* was sighted at eight minutes to one in the afternoon of 16 February 1940. We had been searching since dawn in misty weather which cleared by mid-morning, when the sun came out. It shone upon a sea which appeared to be frozen over a considerable distance from the Norwegian coast. We picked the *Altmark* up about fifteen miles away in Josing Fjord and dived down and read her name in letters a foot high which, though obscured by paint, were clearly visible. We shadowed the ship until HMS *Cossack* arrived on the scene at 2.00 pm, who boarded her and removed the prisoners.'

Below: A Lockheed Hudson VI of No 608 Squadron, Coastal Command operating from Blida, Algeria in early 1943 carries ASV Mk II search radar. It has matt white vertical and gloss white under-surfaces as adopted by Coastal Command in August 1941.

POWERPLANT: Two 820kW (1100hp) Wright Cyclone R-1820-G 102A radial piston engines (Mk I)
SPAN: 19.96m (65ft 6in); Length: 13.51m (44ft 4in)
Max speed: 397km/h (222mph)
TYPICAL ARMAMENT: Twin fixed 0.303in guns forward, twin 0.303in guns in dorsal turret and one 0.303in gun in ventral position; Max bomb load 340kg (750lb)
FIRST AIRCRAFT FLOWN: 10 December 1938
ENTERED RAF SERVICE: May 1939 (Mk I, No 224 Squadron)
LAST RAF SERVICE: August 1945 (Mk III, No 251 Squadron).

BRISTOL BEAUFIGHTER

The Beaufighter was a rugged, functional aeroplane, and looked every inch of it, being able to carry bombs, rockets, cannon, machine-guns and torpedoes. It was developed from the Beaufort, albeit using a new forward fuselage and Bristol Hercules engines. Entering service early in World War II, it served with eighty-four squadrons, proving faster than the Hurricane. The firepower of the Beaufighter was devastating – the Japanese in Burma and Malaya called it the Whispering Death. It proved to be the most heavily armed two-seat fighter bomber in RAF operational use during the war.

Equipped with AI Mk IV radar, the night fighter Beaufighter was a major reason for the Luftwaffe giving up on the Blitz on Britain. Its only operational shortcoming was a tendency to swing on take-off, which the later addition of a larger dorsal fin and dihedral tailplane failed to cure. By June 1943, the most widely-used mark, the Beaufighter X was entering service and became an extremely formidable anti-shipping strike aircraft. ASV radar was carried in a thimble nose radome.

Squadron Leader George McLannahan of No 604 Squadron recalled his Beaufighter experience in 1943, 'As for the Beaufighter as an aircraft, I found the Mk I a strong and powerful machine but very tiring to fly on patrol at night, or on instruments, as it was completely unstable fore and aft. This was virtually cured on the Mk VI. I came on to the Mk VI after flying Mosquitoes and it was like handling a battleship after being used to a destroyer. On this aspect I'll always remember an American in No 153 Squadron who had joined the RAF early on to get into the war. He commented that he felt completely at home in a Beau as he had previously been a truck driver! Rather unfair on the Beau as it was a very fine, solid aircraft. For just one example of this, landing it in a cross-wind was never a problem; once placed properly on the ground it sat there and defied any deviations.'

> **POWERPLANT:** Two 1319kW (1770hp) Bristol Hercules XVII sleeve-vale radial engines (Mk X)
> **SPAN:** 17.63m (57ft 10in); **Length:** 12.6m (41ft 8in)
> **MAX SPEED:** 528km/h (330mph)
> **TYPICAL ARMAMENT:** Four 20mm Hispano cannon fixed underside fuselage and one Vickers K gun aimed by observer; two 454kg (1000lb) bombs, a 728kg (1605lb) torpedo or wing racks for eight rocket projectiles could be carried
> **FIRST AIRCRAFT FLOWN:** 17 July 1939
> **ENTERED RAF SERVICE:** 12 August 1940 (Mk IF, Fighter Interception Unit)
> **LAST RAF SERVICE:** 12 May 1960 (TT10, FEAF, Seletar TT Flight).

Left: A 'Torbeau' loaded with an 18in 1700lb torpedo (known as a 'fish' by RAF crews) in a banking turn. They formed part of the special Beaufighter wing of Coastal Command.

Above: Operating from RAF
North Coates in 1943 this
Beaufighter TFX's rocket projectile
rails are loaded with 25lb SAP
headed rockets, prior to take off
to attack a German convoy.

DOUGLAS BOSTON/ HAVOC

In some respects, the combat career of the Douglas A-20, with its revolutionary nosewheel undercarriage, was much less spectacular than that of many other bombers despite remaining in front-line service throughout the war. Although procured as a bomber, its first application with the RAF was for night fighting and intruder duties as it was capable of carrying the cumbersome early airborne–interception radar. Over one hundred Boston IIs were modified and redesignated Havoc I for this 'Moonfighter' role. It was also the subject of some unusual experiments, including the Turbinlite Havoc with an airborne Helmore searchlight in the nose, while some were used for carrying Long Aerial Mines.

Wing Commander (later Air Commander) A E Clouston of No 1422 Flight recalled the experimental night fighter role, 'The Turbinlite Havoc was accompanied by two Hawker Hurricanes, one flying off each wing. The Turbinlite pilot was supposed to get the target in azimuth near either edge of the beam (width +/- 15°) so that in theory return fire aimed at the light source should pass behind the aircraft.

Below: The first of several British Purchasing Commission orders were placed in February and April 1940, and included 300 DB-7Bs. Here, a Boston, as it was subsequently named, is on test from the Douglas factory prior to acceptance by the RAF.

Right: Boston IIIs were shipped to Britain in the summer of 1941 and these were modified for use as a Blenheim replacement on anti-shipping strikes and daylight raids on continental fringe targets.

Above: Bombs falling from Boston III 'C for Charlie' over Charleroi in France in 1941. While viewed suspiciously at the beginning by RAF pilots, it soon became popular on the squadrons that flew it.

Station keeping was achieved by the use of special illuminated strips on the upper and lower wing surfaces of the Havoc. Much effort was expended on the Turbinlite from the time of its inception in the early days of the Blitz, but it never achieved much real success, apart from its possible value as a deterrent.'

The Boston III proved an excellent bomber on daylight low-level operations over north-west Europe. Flight Lieutenant R A Yates-Earle of No 88 Squadron wrote, 'A typical large-scale action at low level was an attack we made on the large Philips radio works at Eindhoven in Holland. We went in between Dunkirk and Ostend, hit the target and came out over The Hague. The type of formation we used for jobs like that was waves of eight aircraft flying in loose echelon.'

POWERPLANT: Two 1193kW (1600hp) Wright Double-Row Cyclone GR-2600-A5B two-row radial piston engines (Boston III)
SPAN: 18.69m (61ft 4in); Length: 14.32m (47ft 0in)
MAX SPEED: 490km/h (304mph)
TYPICAL ARMAMENT: Four fixed 0.303in guns in nose, twin hand-operated 0.303in guns in dorsal and ventral positions; Max bomb load 909kg (2000lb)
FIRST AIRCRAFT FLOWN: 26 October 1938
ENTERED RAF SERVICE: December 1940 (Havoc I, No 85 Squadron)
LAST RAF SERVICE: July 1946 (Boston V, No 55 Squadron).

HANDLEY PAGE HALIFAX

Below: Based at RAF Graveley, Huntingdon in August 1942, having moved from Linton-on-Ouse, No 35 Squadron was a founder-member of the Path Finder Force (PFF). This squadron Halifax (TL-P) was also one of the PFF's earliest casualties, being lost during a raid on Nuremberg on the night of 28/29 August 1942.

A total of 6176 Halifaxes were built during its six-year production run, indicating its value as a versatile and durable machine. The use of four Merlin engines on the initial aircraft was dictated by the fact that no other engine of comparable power to the ill-fated Rolls-Royce Vulture, as originally contemplated, was then available. No less than four out of ten heavy bombers built in the UK during World War II were Halifaxes. It was not as shapely an aircraft as its Avro Lancaster contemporary, but its deeper, more capacious slab-sided fuselage rendered it suitable for a wide variety of roles. During World War II, the Halifax flew no less than 75,532 bombing sorties during which 227,610 tons of bombs were dropped.

Above: After a four-Halifax mining-laying operation on 2 January 1944, No 433 Squadron (RCAF) at Skipton-on-Swale sent ten of its new Halifax BIIIs, with Bristol Hercules engines, to Magdeburg on 21 January, the squadron's first bombing mission, which continued until 16 January 1945 when the squadron began to convert to Lancasters.

In 1942, in an effort to gain more performance, the mid-upper and nose turrets, together with navigation window blisters, were removed and a nose fairing fitted. Larger fins and rudders were subsequently added to improve stability. Whilst somewhat overshadowed by the Lancaster, it played a very significant part in the heavy bomber operations throughout the war, later with Bristol Hercules engines on the Mks III, VI and VII. The Halifax also served with Coastal Command, and as a glider tug for parachute operations, with experimental electronics work and in dropping weapons and supplies to partisan groups.

Following one of the first missions using H2S radar, the pilot of Halifax W7851/N, Flight Officer Brown reported, 'There was a thin stratocumulus cloud over the target with tops at 5000-8000ft, as a result of which no ground detail could be seen. The target was identified, however, on special equipment and at 02:37 four red flares were dropped at 52°50'

North, 09°09' East from 21,000ft followed three minutes later by sixteen red/green star flares from the same height. Bombs were successfully dropped on the city.'

POWERPLANT: Four 954kW (1280hp) Rolls-Royce Merlin X in-line piston engines (Mk I)
SPAN: 30.12m (98ft 8in); Length: 21.36 (70ft 1in)
MAX SPEED: 426km/h (265mph)
TYPICAL ARMAMENT: Two 0.303in machine guns in dorsal turret and four 0.303in guns in tail turret; Max bomb load 5454kg (12,000lb)
FIRST AIRCRAFT FLOWN: 25 October 1939
ENTERED RAF SERVICE: 23 November 1940 (Mk I, No 35 Squadron)
LAST RAF SERVICE: 17 March 1952 (GRVI, No 224 Squadron).

SHORT STIRLING

Above: Fitted with beam defence guns this Stirling I of No 7 Squadron was lost on operations over Bremen on 26 June 1942.

The Stirling was the first of the RAF's trio of four-engined heavy bombers, and was the only one designed from the outset to be powered by four engines. Because of a restricted wingspan, which was dictated to the manufacturer, the Stirling was unable to reach an acceptable operating altitude with a full bomb load, and the design of the bomb-bay prevented it from carrying any bomb larger than 909kg (2000lb). Despite these failings, the introduction of a four-engined bomber gave a morale boost at an appropriate time. A new departure for aircraft manufacture was the Stirling's modular production. Components were built in over twenty factories. By 1943 the Stirling was flown mainly as a glider tug and transport; it was also used to

carry ECM jamming and 'spoofing' devices for No 100 Group.

A Stirling pilot reported after his first flight, 'My initial impression was of the height above the ground of the pilot, and at first there was a tendency to either fly into the ground upon landing, or to over-compensate and flare out too high.'

An experienced No XV Squadron pilot wrote, 'Any take-off (and landing) required care, the more so if there was any wind from starboard. Operational take-offs with a full load of bombs and fuel called for the greatest care. With the brakes full on and stick held back, the throttles are opened up as far as possible. The entire Stirling airframe begins to judder and vibrate violently, the tail assembly most of all.

1940

POWERPLANT: Four 1230kW (1650hp) Bristol Hercules XVI radial piston engines (Mk III)
SPAN: 30.20m (99ft 1in); Length: 26.60m (87ft 3in)
MAX SPEED: 435km/h (270mph)
TYPICAL ARMAMENT: Two 0.303in guns in nose and dorsal turrets, and four in tail turret; max bomb load 6363kg (14,000lb)
FIRST AIRCRAFT FLOWN: 14 May 1939
ENTERED RAF SERVICE: August 1940 (No 7 Squadron)
LAST RAF SERVICE: July 1946 (Mk V, No 1588 Heavy Freight Flight).

Above: Probably one of the best-known Stirlings of the early war years, N6086 was allocated to No XV Squadron at RAF Wyton on 15 September 1941. The aircraft bears the coat of arms of the MacRobert family and the legend 'MacRobert's Reply'.

Previously hidden by the outboard engines, the wingtips could be seen coming into view as the wings flexed on take-off, taking on the aircraft's weight with the wheels bouncing more and more on the runway, until they lifted clear of the ground.' A senior navigator who flew on many SOE operations with No 620 Squadron, Flight Lieutenant Basil Crocker said, 'I never heard one of those Bristol Hercules engines miss a single beat whilst over enemy territory'.

Left: The Stirling was nightly on the offensive in 1941–42. This bomb trolley load is to be winched up into the cavernous fuselage and wing-root of this Stirling at RAF Waterbeach in 1942.

CONSOLIDATED CATALINA

The twin-engined PBY Catalina became the most numerous flying-boat of World War II. The 'Killer Cat' served with nine RAF squadrons and sank or seriously damaged at least 45 U-boats, while two Catalina skippers were awarded VCs. Though not of outstanding general performance, its long range of some 4,000 miles made the flying boat an essential feature of the Atlantic air cover for Allied shipping. The Catalina enjoyed a better reliability record than the Sunderland, engine failure was almost unknown and it could alight in seas with waves of over six ft high. One remained in the air for more than twenty-six hours during the operations which ended in the sinking of the Bismarck. In winter and bad weather Catalinas frequently returned in darkness to base after an eighteen-hour patrol, and, finding it obscured by fog or low cloud, remained aloft all night until they could land in greater safety at dawn.

Flight Lieutenant John Cruickshank of No 210 Squadron, the only Coastal Command VC to survive the war, recalled his mission, in Catalina JV928 on 17 July 1944, 'We had an unidentified blip on the radar. I sighted the objective – a submarine, fully surfaced and running at about 20kts. Pulling the Catalina into a turn around the U-boat, I began an attack run,

POWERPLANT: Two 894kW (1200hp) Pratt & Whitney Twin Wasp R-1830-S1C3-G radial piston engines
SPAN: 31.72m (104ft 0in); Length: 19.5m (63ft 11in)
MAX SPEED: 314km/h (196mph)
TYPICAL ARMAMENT: One 0.303in gun in bows and two in each side blister and one in 'tunnel' in underside behind hull step; Max bomb load 1818kg (4000lb) or four 148kg (325lb) depth charges
FIRST AIRCRAFT FLOWN: 21 March 1935 (XPBY-1)
ENTERED RAF SERVICE: March 1941 (Mk I, No 240 Squadron)
LAST RAF SERVICE: October 1945 (Mk IV, No 240 Squadron).

descending from 1000 to 50ft. My nose gunner began splashing fire against the conning tower. Everybody ready? – in we go – we made a perfect run in at low level but when we were almost on top of the U-boat, a shell burst in the aircraft, our navigator was killed and I was seriously wounded. The depth charges were released and it was a perfect straddle. The attack was accurate and U–347, on only its second war patrol, was sunk.'

Left: No 209 Squadron left for East Africa in March 1942 and flew patrols over the Indian Ocean for the rest of the war. Here a Catalina 1 is taking off from its base at Kipevu, Mombassa in 1944.

Right: The amphibious PBY-5A Catalina VI was a late variant that had a taller fin and rudder and a number of improvements to the hull and wingtip floats. It also had a bigger fuel capacity with a correspondingly higher all-up-weight and longer range. The aircraft photographed is owned by Plain Sailing Air Displays.

CONSOLIDATED LIBERATOR

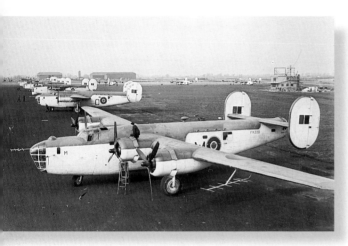

In its maritime role, the B-24 Liberator had a range of 3685km (2290 miles) and it was this particular asset which enabled RAF Coastal Command to close the critical 'Atlantic Gap' being dominated by the German U-boats. A total of 2000 Liberators were received by the RAF, and their long range with twelve-and-a-half hours endurance, large load capacity and use of the homing torpedo, contributed to significant German losses. They were also part of the Atlantic Ferry service. Later Liberators

were gradually equipped with ASV radar aerials, a four 20mm cannon belly pack instead of a nose turret, Leigh Lights and H2S radar.

Gradually the presence of Liberators flying from Iceland, Scotland and Northern Ireland forced the new long-range U-boats to move further south, to the west coast of Africa. Success with new depth charges filled with Torpex (set to explode 25ft below the surface) forced U-boats to remain submerged for much longer periods, thereby severely reducing their patrol endurance.

Captain Eric 'Winkle' Brown, RN tested the Liberator against the Halifax and Lancaster at Farnborough in 1944. He reported on its general handling characteristics, 'Although the Liberator appeared on the scene some four years after the Flying Fortress, it had only a very small advantage in speed or range over the B-17 and was more complicated to fly and handled less well. However, it had more development potential, and 19,203 were built, more than any other single type of American aircraft. It unquestionably proved a boon to Coastal Command and, although I have never heard any pilot wax lyrical about its flying qualities, it proved to be a good solid performer, or as an ex-Liberator pilot put it, a grand old warrior. That makes a fitting epitaph for the B-24.'

POWERPLANT:
Four 895kW (1200hp) Pratt & Whitney Twin Wasp R-1830-43 two-row radial piston engines (Mk VI)
SPAN: 33.5m (110ft 0in); Length: 20.47m (67ft 1in)
MAX SPEED: 467km/h (290mph)
TYPICAL ARMAMENT:
Twin 0.50in guns in nose, dorsal and tail turrets, plus one 0.50in gun in ventral turret and at each waist position; max bomb load, 3636kg (8000lb)
FIRST AIRCRAFT FLOWN: 29 December 1939 (XB-24)
ENTERED RAF SERVICE: June 1941 (Mk I, No 120 Squadron)
LAST RAF SERVICE: June 1947 (GRVIII, No 203 Squadron).

Above: The long range of the Consolidated Liberator made it of special value to the RAF both as a convoy escort/anti-submarine aircraft and later as a bomber in the Far East. No 120 Squadron's GR IIIs – depicted at their Aldergrove base – are fitted with tell-tale Yagi aerials of ASV radar and carried bombs and depth charges.

Right: Liberator GRVI of No 547 Squadron at RAF Leuchars, Fife late 1944. This version had a maximum endurance of over twelve hours and to obtain the range defensive armament was drastically reduced.

De HAVILLAND MOSQUITO

The DH98 Mosquito relied for its defence on its ability to outpace any intercepting fighter. With two Merlin engines, extreme aerodynamic cleanliness and a high power-to-weight ratio, the performance of the 'Wooden Wonder' surpassed that of any other operational aircraft. Aesthetically, the Mosquito was one of the most appealing combat aircraft designs of World War II, and it possessed delightful flying characteristics.

The 'Mossie' filled almost every front-line requirement in all theatres of war. It became the RAF's premier long-range photographic reconnaissance aircraft – in 1943 alone, No 1 PRU at

POWERPLANT: Two 1275kW (1710hp) Rolls-Royce Merlin 114A in-line piston engines (Mk 35)
SPAN: 16.51m (54ft 2in); Length: 12.64m (41ft 6in)
MAX SPEED: 681km/h (422mph)
Typical armament: Bomber – no defensive guns; max bomb load 1818kg (4000lb). Fighter – Four 20mm and four 0.303in guns forward; eight rocket projectiles under the wings (Mk XXX)
FIRST AIRCRAFT FLOWN: 25 November 1940
ENTERED RAF SERVICE: November 1941 (Mk IV, No 105 Squadron)
LAST RAF SERVICE: 1963 (T3/TT35, Nos 3 and 4 CAACUs).

Right: This Mosquito was owned by British Aerospace and displayed at airshows until 1995.

Far Right: The Mosquito found its métier in many roles. One of the least known, but most effective, was to supplement the Beaufighter in shipping strikes with bombs and rockets in Coastal Command as seen on this Mosquito BVI.

Overleaf: The most ubiquitous military aircraft of all time, the Mosquito was conceived as a 'bomber with fighter speed' and was built of wood allowing conservation of other materials likely to be in short supply during wartime.

Benson dispatched some 3000 sorties all over Europe, and the type continued in the role well after the war. Replacing the Blenheim in No 2 Group, Bomber Command, the Mosquito IV squadrons worked tirelessly and extremely successfully on daylight raids in 1942–43, with the lowest loss rate of any aircraft involved in the campaign. Subsequently, alongside night bomber operations, 'Mossies' became the mainstay of the Pathfinder Force.

Group Captain Leonard Cheshire VC recalled the target marking for No 617 Squadron in his Mosquito. 'It was 14 June 1944 and the invasion was going well. Nevertheless, the Allies had no great desire to allow E-boats to sink the supply ships, so the pens were to be attacked. As I reached the coast, I pushed the Mosquito down and hurtled through a curtain of ack-ack to the heart of the harbour, and

there tied up in the neat concrete bays, were fifteen E-boats. No amount of ground fire could deter me now, not with a target like this. Down, deadly accurate, went my red marker flares. Overhead, in the gloaming, protected by Spitfires, our massive Lancasters droned in. Then tallboy after tallboy smashed down on to those twinkling spots of red that were my flares.'

The role of the Mosquito as a night-fighter was significant, its radar equipment being progressively upgraded through to the NF38, the last Mosquito produced in 1950. The Mk VI was the most widely used variant, being used as a fighter–bomber. Fighter Command's most famous Mosquito mission was the attack on the Amiens jail in February 1944, which allowed 258 French Resistance prisoners to escape. Coastal Command Mosquitos went into action against enemy shipping, replacing Beaufighters.

HAWKER TYPHOON

In the late 1930s, the Air Ministry called for new interceptor fighters to succeed the Hurricane and Spitfire, with a speed increase of at least 100mph, and with much heavier armament, twelve Browning machine guns or four 20mm cannon. The Air Ministry stipulated two new 24-cylinder engines – the Napier Sabre and Rolls-Royce Vulture X – but both were troublesome. The former was eventually selected to power the Typhoon, the RAF's first 400mph fighter on service entry with No 56 Squadron at Duxford in September 1941.

Once it had overcome initial engine and structural problems, the Typhoon went on to achieve great success and add considerably to the art of ground attack which had almost been forgotten since World War I. Sweeps over occupied Europe began in 1942, attacking airfields and the enemy's means of communication, most famously trains. It became the backbone of the 2nd Tactical Air Force fighter–bomber wings in support of the advance through Northern France and the Low Countries. The work of the Typhoon squadrons (by now rocket-armed in preparation for, during and after D-Day) was significant.

Looking back, Roland Beamont described his first Typhoon flight, 'At first sight the Typhoon was a heavy-looking, rather cumbersome aeroplane. Nevertheless, at closer acquaintance it was seen to be an immensely rugged aeroplane with a thick, high-lift wing of generous area with an impressive Napier

Below: Typhoons squadrons were among the first Allied aircraft to operate from Advanced Landing Grounds (ALGs) in Normandy after D-Day. Here ground crew load rockets on a cannon armed Typhoon.

Sabre engine of almost twice the power of the Merlin – it gave an immediate impression of power and strength.'

Squadron Leader (later Air Marshal) Denis Crowley Milling formed the first Typhoon fighter–bomber squadron, No 181 (known as 'Bomphoons'). He recalled, 'As you dived down, you could look behind and see the heavy flak bursting to the rear. We developed a pretty good accuracy; on one occasion one of my bombs actually burst under an enemy aircraft as it was touching down. The whole essence of the operation was to hit and then get out fast; it did not pay to hang around.'

Above: With a full load of 60lb rockets a Typhoon of No 181 Squadron takes off from Eindhoven in late 1944.

Right: As a cannon-armed successor to the Hurricane, the Hawker Typhoon entered service in September 1941. Typhoons performed best at low levels and carried out devastating attacks on German columns in the Falaise gap during August 1944, using rocket projectiles as well as bombs.

POWERPLANT: One 1640kW (2200hp) Napier Sabre IIB in-line piston engine
SPAN: 12.67m (47ft 7in); Length: 9.73m (31ft 11in)
MAX SPEED: (664km/h) 412mph
TYPICAL ARMAMENT: Four 20mm Hispano cannon; provision for two 455kg (1,000lb) bombs and up to sixteen 27.3kg (60lb) three-inch rocket projectiles
FIRST AIRCRAFT FLOWN: 24 February 1940
ENTERED RAF SERVICE: August 1941 (Mk I, No 56 Squadron)
LAST RAF SERVICE:
September 1945 (Mk IB, No 609 Squadron).

AVRO LANCASTER

The four-engined Lancaster was a direct descendant of the ill-fated Manchester, flying for the first time from the Avro factory airfield at Woodford in January 1941, with deliveries of production examples to No 44 Squadron at Waddington commencing eight months later. The unit went into battle with its new Lancaster Is early in 1942, and the cycle of raids intensified still further through that year, with deliveries of the new bomber to other squadrons.

Bomber Command created No 5 Group entirely equipped with Lancasters. It achieved many important feats – it was the first aircraft type to fly Pathfinder missions (August 1942); the first to carry 3636kg (8000lb) bombs (April 1943); first to carry a 5455kg (12,000lb) bomb (September 1943) and the 5455kg (12,000lb) 'Tallboy' deep penetration bomb (July 1944), and the mammoth 10,000kg (22,000lb) bomb (March 1945). Perhaps the most famous of all Lancaster raids was carried out by No 617 Squadron

Left: Built by Vickers Armstrong in 1944 at Chester, this sole UK airworthy Lancaster example, is operated by the Battle of Britain Memorial Flight at RAF Coningsby. It was taken on charge by the RAF's Historical Branch in October 1963 and has been with the BBMF since 1965.

Above: The foreground bombs are 4000lb thin-cased 'cookies' – blast-bombs, and the Lancaster is a very early one here with No 83 Squadron at RAF Wyton in 1942. The original No 44 Squadron markings are still visible.

on the Möhne and Eder Dams – Operation *Chastise* – in May 1943. The 'Lanc' achieved further fame by the sinking of the *Tirpitz* in November 1944 and playing the major part in the raid on the German experimental rocket base at Peenemunde in August 1943. Of the 32 VCs awarded to RAF personnel during World War II, ten were given to Lancaster aircrew.

Lancasters not only made the major contribution to Bomber Command's night offensive on Germany, they also helped to turn the scales in the great land battles of 1944 by bombing German armies in the field. A total of 7377 Lancasters were built, flying 156,318 sorties and dropping 608,613 tons of bombs but 3345 were lost in action. By 1945 there were fifty-six squadrons operational on Lancasters. With the departure of Lend-Lease Liberators from the RAF in 1945, the Lancaster became the principal land-based maritime reconnaissance aircraft of Coastal Command, until finally superseded by the Neptune and Shackleton in early 1954.

Group Captain Leonard Cheshire VC extolled the virtues of Lancasters of No 617 Squadron, 'We have now achieved an accuracy with the Lancaster

Right: BBMF Lancaster PA474 is currently in the markings of W4964 'WS-J', Johnie Walker, an aircraft of No IX Squadron. This aircraft took part in the first attack on the *Tirpitz* from Russia and flew over one hundred operational sorties, as can be seen from the nose-art seen here.

Below: During the winter of 1995/96 the BBMF Lancaster received a brand new main spar which will extend its life well into the next millennium.

City of Lincoln

such that, from 20,000ft we can guarantee two direct hits on any target, fifteen per cent of their bombs within 25 yds of the centre of the target, and seventy-five per cent of their bombs within 80 yds of it. This is precision undreamed of in the past.'

Left: BBMF Lancaster PA474 is one of only two Lancasters remaining in air-worthy condition – the other being in Canada. The bomber joined the flight in November 1973.

POWERPLANT: Four 1088kW (1460hp) Rolls-Royce Merlin 20 or 22 in-line piston engines (Mk I)
SPAN: 31.10m (102ft 0in); Length: 21.10m (69ft 4in)
MAX SPEED: 462km/h (287mph)
TYPICAL ARMAMENT: Nose and dorsal turrets with two 0.303in Brownings and tail turret with four 0.303in Brownings. Normal bomb load 6350kg (14,000lb)
FIRST AIRCRAFT FLOWN: 9 January 1941
ENTERED RAF SERVICE: September 1941 (Mk I, No 44 Squadron)
LAST RAF SERVICE: February 1954 (MR3, No 38 Squadron).

NORTH AMERICAN MITCHELL

By 1941 the strategic bomber offensive had shifted to night operations by Bomber Command heavy and medium bombers, but one entire group – No 2 – still exclusively flew daylight operations. The third of a trio of American 'twins' to join this Group was the Mitchell (the first two being the Boston and Ventura). The main version of the Mitchell supplied to the RAF was the Mk II, counterpart of the USAAF's B-25C and D, of which 542 were received. Primary missions of the Mitchells were to be the intruder Circus and Ramrod operations, with a secondary shipping attack role.

The final RAF version was the B-25J Mitchell III, of which 269 were received, flying their first operational missions in January 1943. They operated with the 2nd Tactical Air Force as close-support

bombers, as the Allied armies advanced through France and the Low Countries. No 98 Squadron's Mitchells bombed German territory for the first time in September 1944. Over the next six months they were replaced by Mosquito XVI bombers, and Mitchells flew their last operation with 2nd TAF on 2 May 1945.

In a critical assessment, test pilot Captain Eric 'Winkle' Brown, RN reported, 'My first impression of the B-25 was how functional and business-like it looked with its angular shape, gull wings, large engines, tricycle undercarriage and its bristling guns. The cockpit is surprisingly compact, with a fairly orderly layout and a reasonable view ahead. The take-off was perhaps, the most exciting feature of the Mitchell, as the acceleration was so impressive. The

Above: Based at Gilze Rijen, Netherlands in late 1944, these Mitchell IIs of No 226 Squadron were operating in support of advancing Allied armies in the tactical support role. they still retained their D-Day black and white striping due to pressure of operations which prevented their removal.

Below: This Mitchell is owned and operated since 1990 by the 'Duke of Brabant Air Force' based in the Netherlands. Finished in the colour scheme of No 320 (Dutch) Squadron when based with No 2 Group at Melsbroek in late 1944, it is currently displayed at airshows throughout Europe.

1942

POWERPLANT: Two 1267kW (1700hp) Wright Double-Row Cyclone GR-2600-13 radial engines (Mk II)
SPAN: 20.57m (67ft 6.75in); Length: 16.48m (54ft 1in)
MAX SPEED: 580km/h (315mph)
TYPICAL ARMAMENT: Two 0.50in guns in each of dorsal and ventral positions and one 0.30in in nose; max bomb load 1818kg (4000lb)
FIRST AIRCRAFT FLOWN: 19 August 1940
ENTERED RAF SERVICE: September 1942 (MkI, Nos 98 and 180 Squadrons)
LAST RAF SERVICE: November 1945 (MkIII, No 98 Squadron).

elevators are very powerful in raising the nosewheel, and unstick takes place at 95mph in a very short distance. In my opinion the Mitchell was probably the most versatile medium bomber of the Second World War. It was not as fast as the Boston, but it carried more bombs and was more heavily armed for its defence. However, for sheer flying exhilaration I preferred the Boston.'

Below: Mitchell IIs were delivered to Nos 98 and 180 Squadrons at RAF West Raynham in September 1942, and flew their first operation on 22 January 1943 in an attack on oil refineries in Belgium.

NORTH AMERICAN MUSTANG

In January 1940 North American undertook to design a new fighter to British requirements, taking into account early lessons from aerial combat over Europe. The company accepted a 120-day limit for constructing a prototype with an in-line engine and the then standard British armament of eight machine guns. The resulting P-51 Mustang was superior to any contemporary US fighter, using a laminar-flow wing for the first time and incorporating a smooth nose design with the radiator located further back than usual.

In May 1942 Wing Commander Ian Campbell-Orde, commanding the Air Fighting Development Unit at Duxford appraised the first RAF Mustang I, 'It is faster than the Spitfire VB at all heights up to 25,000ft and compares favourably in manoeuvrability. It can out-dive the Spitfire with ease, but has an inferior rate of climb. The aircraft is pleasant to fly in formation. It has a wide speed range, but owing to its clean lines, deceleration is slow. The aircraft, being extremely stable, is very easy to fly on instruments and it can be trimmed to fly "hands and feet off" in level flight or when climbing or diving.'

These initial Allison-engined Mustang Is were accepted by the RAF in October 1941, but powerplant performance difficulties saw them operating on army co-operation sorties rather than as fighters. However, the Mustang III and IV were powered by a Packard-built Merlin engine and rapidly became significant Fighter Command assets. RAF Mustang III operations commenced in December 1943 escorting bomber formations. A transfer to the 2nd Tactical Air Force saw the aircraft flying fighter–bomber sorties, but in late 1944 they rejoined Fighter Command in the UK, being used against the V1 flying bombs (shooting 232 down). Subsequently, the main role of the Mustang units was as fighter escorts for Bomber Command's daylight operations over Germany, Coastal Command's shipping strikes off Norway and precision raids with Mosquitos. They also operated with the Desert Air Force in Italy. Mustang IVs (the USAAF P-51D variant) entered service in March 1945 and were the first RAF aircraft to greet Russian aircraft over Berlin. Post-war they were used in Cyprus until replaced by Tempest VIs in 1947.

POWERPLANT: One 1252kW (1680hp) Packard-built Rolls-Royce Merlin V-1650-7 in-line piston engine (MkIII)
SPAN: 11.29m (37ft 0in); Length: 9.81m (32ft 2in)
MAX SPEED: 712km/h (442mph)
Typical armament: Four 0.50in guns and provision for 454kg (1000lb) of bombs
FIRST AIRCRAFT FLOWN: 26 October 1940
ENTERED SERVICE: 5 May 1942 (MkI, No 26 Squadron)
LAST RAF SERVICE: February 1947 (MkIV, No 213 Squadron).

Left: One of the outstanding fighters of World War II, a design that was to prove indispensable and little short of a war-winner, the Mustang was conceived to a British requirement.

Right: A North American Mustang IV, in formation with a Spitfire and Kittyhawk. In early 1945 Mustang IVs began to appear in the Mediterranean theatre and the Commonwealth units.

Above: The prototype York C1 was subsequently converted as the first – and only – C2, with four Bristol Hercules engines. Though more powerful than the Merlin engines, the Hercules was a heavier engine and there was no gain in performance.

AVRO YORK

The Avro York first flew as a private venture aircraft in July 1942. It was a transport development of the Lancaster, using the same undercarriage and engines, but introduced an entirely new fuselage with twice the cubic capacity. The Lancaster had priority on the production lines, resulting in relatively few of the 203 Yorks eventually built flying before the end of the war. These were mostly VIP aircraft, whose regular passengers included Winston Churchill, Lord Louis Mountbatten and Field Marshal Jan Smuts.

The first RAF Transport Command squadron to operate the York was No 511 at Lyneham from November 1943. The unit concentrated on long-range operations, and eventually thirteen Yorks were allocated to 'A' Flight. However, it did not enter general service with RAF transport squadrons until 1945.

By the start of the Berlin Airlift in 1948, the RAF had six York squadrons, all of which took part in Operations *Plainfare* and *Vittles*. They made over 29,000 flights to the German capital and carried some 230,000 tons of supplies – nearly half the total contribution by the RAF. By 1949 the Handley Page Hastings was entering service with Transport Command and eventually replaced the York.

Writing about his experience flying on the Airlift, an RAF York pilot described how the aircraft and personnel were pushed to the limit, 'To begin with, the Yorks were operated at a maximum loaded weight of 27,216kg (60,000lb). On 16 July their landing weight was increased to 29,484kg (65,000lb) on receipt of HQ Transport Command authority, and the maximum take-off weight went up to 30,391kg (67,000lb). This gave a payload of 7484kg (16,500lb) for the York freighter, and 6804kg (15,000lb) for the passenger/freighter. We experienced difficulty in loading the passenger/freighter version because of the small size of the door and its position under the wing. The original estimate for the turn-round for York aircraft at base was two hours, but after a few days of operations it was found that two-and-a-half hours was the average time required. The usual time spent on the ground by the Yorks at Gatow was just forty-five minutes.'

Below: Avro Yorks on Gatow's apron during the Berlin Airlift of 1949. The identity number on the tail allowed easy recognition once on the ground. The aircraft were marshalled in front of the hangars, where a German labour force unloaded them. Unloading time averaged out at about ten minutes.

POWERPLANT: Four 954kW (1280hp) Rolls-Royce Merlin 22 or 24 in-line piston engines
SPAN: 31.0m (102ft 0in); **Length:** 23.9m (78ft 6in)
MAX SPEED: 480km/h (298mph)
ACCOMMODATION: Crew of five; twenty-four passengers or 7484kg (16,500lb) freight
FIRST AIRCRAFT FLOWN: 5 July 1942
ENTERED RAF SERVICE: May 1943 (No 24 Squadron)
LAST RAF SERVICE: 1957 (FEAF Communications).

DOUGLAS DAKOTA

Delivery of the first Douglas C-47 for the RAF took place on 9 January 1943, and the type was named Dakota (usually abbreviated to 'Dak'), the name by which all C-47s and DC-3s have been universally known ever since. The newly-delivered RAF Dakotas were soon in action in Burma, dropping supplies to British Army troops operating well behind Japanese lines. On D-Day, five squadrons contributed 108 Dakotas to carry the Parachute Brigade to Normandy, each joined by two Horsa gliders with supplies. The next major operations in Europe involving Dakotas were the ill-fated airborne landings, during Operation *Market Garden*, in September 1944. Rather more successful was the final airborne assault of the war, Operation *Varsity* on 24 March 1945, to secure bridgeheads across the Rhine in which seven RAF Dakotas were lost.

Many RAF Dakotas were lost at Arnhem, and the final flight of Flight Lieutenant David Lord of No 271 Squadron, for which he received the posthumous award of the Victoria Cross, exemplifies the bravery of the transport crews. It was gazetted in November 1945. 'Lord's aircraft was one of seventeen carrying ammunition panniers to be dropped on the outskirts of Arnhem. Nearing the target at 1500ft it came under heavy anti-aircraft fire, being hit twice in the wing and having its starboard engine set on fire. With only three minutes to go before the drop, and with the engine ablaze, Lord descended to 900ft and came under even heavier fire. Damage to the roller track in the Dakota caused the panniers to jam and the crew had to manhandle them through the doorway. The delay resulted in two panniers still being in position, so Lord took the aircraft round for a second run over the drop zone. By now, at only 600ft and well ablaze, the Dakota was being shot to pieces but Lord held it straight and ordered the crew to bail out. Before they could do so the wing detached and the Dakota crashed, with no survivors.'

The Dakota continued in RAF service well after World War II. Nine squadrons contributed aircraft to the Berlin Airlift in 1948–49, while the counter-insurgency campaign in Malaya, starting in 1956, saw Dakotas being used for leaflet-dropping and sky-shouting. It was not until 1970 that the last RAF Dakota was retired from active service.

POWERPLANT: Two 894kW (1200hp) Pratt & Whitney Twin Wasp R-1830-92 radial piston engines
SPAN: 28.96m (95ft 0in); Length: 19.64m (64ft 5in)
MAX SPEED: 370km/h (230mph)
ACCOMMODATION: Crew of three; room for 28 troops
FIRST AIRCRAFT FLOWN: 17 December 1935 (DC-3)
ENTERED RAF SERVICE: 1942 (DC-3, No 31 Squadron); March 1943 (Dakota I, No 24 Squadron)
LAST RAF SERVICE: 1 April 1970 (C4, Allied Air Forces Northern Europe).

HAWKER TEMPEST

Right: A formation of Tempest Vs from the RAF Central Fighter Establishment at RAF West Raynham in 1945, where most of the RAF's trials and evaluations on fighter-type aircraft were conducted. The nearest aircraft has eight of the lengthened rocket rails fitted.

Below: The Tempest was one of many Allied aircraft to have 'invasion stripes' on the underside of the fuselage only. On D-Day there were three squadrons of Tempest Vs – Nos 3, 56 and 486.

The Tempest, developed from the Typhoon, featured the new, thin-section laminar-flow wing, elliptical in plan, and a lengthened fuselage to accommodate the fuel tanks moved from the wings. The thinner and cleaner wing gave the Tempest a considerable edge over contemporary fighters in dive speed and lateral control, and it was the first Allied fighter to achieve 500mph. Three main marks were produced – the Tempest V and VI used the Napier Sabre engine, while the Tempest II was powered by the Bristol Centaurus.

The Tempest V was first into service in April 1944, starting operations with strafing and interdiction sorties in Northern France but then progressing most successfully to the effort to combat the V1 flying bomb menace. 638 V1s were to be destroyed by the fast Tempests – Bob Cole of No 3

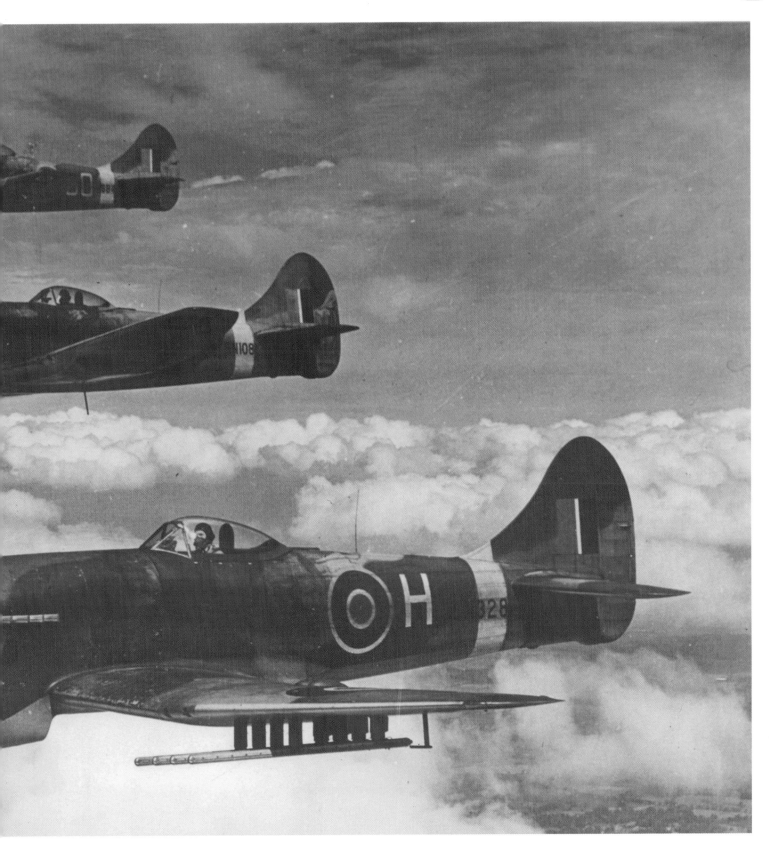

Left: One of the first units to receive the Tempest was No 501 (RAuxAF) Squadron at RAF Manston, three of whose Mk V Series 2 aircraft are pictured. The squadron was in action against V1 flying bombs three days after converting to the type in August 1944, and specialized in night interceptions: the CO alone got six doodle-bugs.

POWERPLANT: One 1640kW (2200hp) Napier Sabre IIB in-line piston engine (MkV)
SPAN: 12.5m (41ft 0in); **Length:** 10.86m (33ft 8in)
MAX SPEED: 688km/h (442mph)
TYPICAL ARMAMENT: Four 20mm cannon; provision to carry up to 909kg (2,000lb) of bombs or eight rocket projectiles
FIRST AIRCRAFT FLOWN: 2 September 1942 (MkV)
ENTERED RAF SERVICE: April 1944 (MkV, No 3 Squadron)
LAST RAF SERVICE: July 1955 (TT5, No 233 OCU).

Squadron, who shot down twenty-two V1s in a four-week period said, 'The Tempest quickly established itself as the most formidable low and medium altitude British fighter and the most capable type of all against the flying bomb.' Wing Commander Roland Beamont (OC of the first Tempest Wing) also reported: 'When intercepting the V1 with the Tempest there was nothing by which to judge distance, except a light which got progressively bigger and more dazzling. It was not easy to get into an effective firing range without suddenly overshooting and possibly even running into the target... the wake of the V1 was felt in the Tempest... then, with the gunsight centred directly on the exhaust flame, a long burst was generally enough to deal with it.'

The top speed of the Tempest V also stood it in good stead when twelve squadrons joined the 2nd Tactical Air Force for the final assault on Germany. In combat with German jets, Tempest pilots shot down twenty Me262s. The other two versions were used post-war – the VI was a tropicalized version, while the more powerful Centaurus-engined Tempest II, also served mainly in Germany and the Far East.

GLOSTER METEOR

Below: In 1947, with a 600mph fighter becoming operational in rapidly mounting numbers in RAF squadrons and overseas, training was beginning to be a vast problem. Thus the two-seat Meteor T7 was developed.

Following the initial test work carried out by Frank Whittle and Power Jets, which led to Gloster's E28/39 test aircraft becoming the first British jet to fly in 1942, the Meteor was the first jet-engined aircraft to enter full production operational service with any air force in the world. From mid-1944 it served for a decade as the RAF's principal fighter aircraft, being used as an interceptor, night fighter, ground-attack aircraft and trainer with thirty-two squadrons and training units.

Nicknamed the 'Meatbox', the Meteor was built in thirty-four sub-types, with seventeen different types of power units. Meteor Is flying with No 616 Squadron in 1944, claimed their first kills against the V1 flying bombs, and the Meteor III (which used the new Derwent turbojet) became the first jet type to see action with the Allies in the 2nd Tactical Air Force in Europe. After the war Meteor F4s replaced the earlier marks, being followed into service by the F8, the most numerous Meteor fighter derivative, which was the RAF's standard day-fighter until Hunters arrived in quantity. Another significant version was the T7, the service's first jet trainer.

Former Hawker Siddeley test pilot Duncan Simpson remembers his step up from training on the Harvard to the Meteor T7, 'From students' and instructors' points of view the two-seat Meteor Mk 7 was a superb vehicle. View from the front cockpit was

135

1944

POWERPLANT: Two 16.03kN (3600lb st) Rolls-Royce Derwent 8 turbojets (F8)
SPAN: 11.32m (37ft 2in); **Length:** 13.58m (44ft 7in)
MAX SPEED: 964km/h (598mph)
TYPICAL ARMAMENT: Four 20mm Hispano cannon in nose (F8)
FIRST AIRCRAFT FLOWN: 5 March 1943
ENTERED RAF SERVICE: 12 July 1944 (MkI, No 616 Squadron)
LAST RAF SERVICE: 1983 (F8, No 1 TWU).

Above: In the autumn of 1945 this Gloster Meteor IV of the RAF High Speed Flight was given a special high-speed finish for an attack on the world's speed record. On 7 November Group Captain H J Wilson flew the aircraft, named *Britannia*, and set a new record of 606mph at Herne Bay.

good, particularly forward, and from the instructor's rear seat it was adequate, despite the amount of metalwork in the massive hood, which opened sideways. Both cockpits were spacious and reasonably well laid out... Compared to the Harvard, the Meteor environment was spectacularly different.'

Produced by Armstrong Whitworth, the Meteor night fighter, with its extended radar nose, was the

first jet aircraft to take up this role in the RAF. The NF11 came into use in late 1950, systems improvements going on to produce the NF12 and then the NF14, the last RAF Meteors in front-line squadron service. Meteors continued to be used, modified for such roles as target tugs, forward air control and continuation trainers, until 1983.

Left: The first Meteor NF11 night fighter was flown in May 1950 and has a lengthened di-electric nose containing the scanner for the Mk10 AI radar. This last remaining airworthy example is owned, and operated, by Jet Heritage at Bournemouth.

Right: Glosters built this two-seat T7, with a pupil and instructor seated in tandem in unpressurized cockpits under a long heavy-framed canopy.

POST
WORLD
WAR II

AVRO LINCOLN

Below: An Avro Lincoln II (FE) of No 57 Squadron at RAF East Kirkby on 26 October 1945. The Lincoln was to have been part of the `Tiger Force' in the Far East and was finished with white upper surfaces to reflect heat, particularly from wing fuel tanks.

The Lincoln was the last of the Avro family of heavy bombers and the last piston-engined bomber to serve with the RAF. Although something of a stop-gap aircraft, it proved a reliable workhorse. Developed from the Lancaster, it was originally designed to be used by the Allied Tiger Force in the Pacific, but with the end of World War II it was not deployed to the Far East, and thus became

the main equipment (alongside the Boeing Washington) of Bomber Command from 1945-55, bridging the gap between the Lancaster and the arrival of the four-jet V-bombers. It saw active service with detachments abroad from January 1947 to the mid-1950s, flying operations against terrorists in Malaya, the Mau Mau in Kenya and through 1956 in Aden.

The Lincoln was a natural extension of the basic

Left: Developed from the Lancaster the Lincoln was the last piston-engined bomber to be used by the RAF and became the main workhouse for the RAF squadrons in the immediate post-war years.

Lancaster formula to carry heavy loads further. It had increased span for operation at greater heights with heavier loads of bombs and fuel. The Merlin engines had two-stage blowers and four-blade propellers. The first Lincoln Trials Flight of No 57 Squadron reported, 'Considerable flexing of the wings, particularly at the tips - but the manufacturers had allowed for an eight-foot movement.' Lincolns made a visit to the USAF SAC bombing competition in America, and whilst refuelling in Iceland the type fascinated onlookers. One USAF pilot remarked, 'You'll never get across the Atlantic in that!' The Americans also thought the RAF crews looked much too young to be capable of flying heavy bombers, while also they could not quite comprehend how an NCO pilot could captain a crew which included officers.

A No 97 Squadron pilot remarked, 'I have a lasting affection for the Lincoln. It is one of the two aircraft for which I had an immediate affinity as soon as I put my hands on it.'

POWERPLANT: Four 1304kW (1750hp) Rolls-Royce Merlin 85A in-line piston engines
SPAN: 36.6m (120ft 0in); Length: 23.85m (78ft 3.5in)
MAX SPEED: 475km/h (295mph)
TYPICAL ARMAMENT: Max bomb load 6364kg (14,000lb); two 0.50in machine guns in nose and tail turrets; two 20mm cannon in mid-upper turret.
FIRST AIRCRAFT FLOWN: 9 June 1944
ENTERED RAF SERVICE: August 1945 (No 57 Squadron)
LAST RAF SERVICE: May 1963 (B2, No 151 Squadron).

De HAVILLAND VAMPIRE

The DH Vampire, known initially as the Spidercrab, was the second type of jet fighter to enter service with the RAF, but was too late to see war service. It featured a short central nacelle, built of wood with a pressurized cockpit forward of the engine, with wing-root inlets and short jet pipe, the tail being carried on twin booms with the tailplane above the jet efflux. It was the first Allied aircraft to exceed 500mph in level flight.

The total production of Vampires was 3206, greater than any other post-war British aircraft. The F1 entered service in April 1946, but was soon supplanted by the F3 with a different tail design and better performance. On 1 July 1948 six Vampire F3s of No 54 Squadron departed from RAF Odiham to make the first ever crossing of the Atlantic by jet-powered aircraft, beating the USAF in their F-80 Shooting Stars by a couple of weeks. The Vampire's role was extended to that of a fighter–bomber with the FB5, and by 1951 it was in widespread service with both the Middle and Far East Air Forces – the FB9 was subsequently developed for tropical operations.

The two-seat Vampire T11, the first jet aircraft to

Below and right: With its excellent performance and fire power, strong construction and ease of maintenance, the Vampire proved ideal for conditions in the UK and overseas.

Above: The introduction into service of the de Havilland Vampire T11 brought about a revolution in RAF flying training. For the first time pilots were able to qualify on a jet aircraft, having side-by-side seating, dual controls and dual instrumentation. With a Meteor T7, this Vampire T11 was flown by the RAF s Vintage Pair display team.

be used by the RAF for advanced flying training outlasted all other marks. Over 700 were delivered, on which over 3000 RAF pilots gained their 'wings' between 1952 and 1967. Chris Ashworth, a Vampire T11 instructor, recalled that, 'It was very easy to start, taxi, take-off and land. The view from the cockpit was good and the controls well co-ordinated. The Vampire was an excellent trainer because it needed a light touch to be flown accurately, a useful cross-country machine because it was comparatively economical on fuel, and quite good for aerobatics, especially in the looping plane. During formation flying, much more anticipation was required than on propeller-driven aeroplanes, both to catch up and slow down. Circuit flying was straightforward unless it was raining. Then it could be difficult to see forward through the flat windscreen, especially at night. Perhaps one of the most off-putting features was the strange noise sometimes produced by the Goblin!'

POWERPLANT: One 14.9kN (3350lb st) de Havilland Goblin DGiv3 turbojet (FB9)
SPAN: 11.58m (38ft 0in); Length: 9.37m (30ft 9in)
MAX SPEED: 883km/h (548mph)
TYPICAL ARMAMENT: Four 20mm guns and provision for up to 909kg (2000lb) of bombs or rockets under wings
FIRST AIRCRAFT FLOWN: 20 September 1943
ENTERED RAF SERVICE: April 1946 (F1, No 247 Squadron)
LAST RAF SERVICE: December 1971 (T11, No 3/4 CAACU).

HANDLEY PAGE HASTINGS

The Hastings replaced the Avro York as the standard long-range RAF transport. On 1 November 1948, the RAF's contribution to the Berlin Airlift received a considerable boost with the arrival at Schleswigland of the first Hastings C1 of Dishforth-based No 47 Squadron. It could carry an eight-ton payload at a cruising speed of a little over 483km/h (300mph). In all three Hastings squadrons were employed on the Airlift. The Hastings C2 was introduced in late 1950 and had more powerful engines, a larger span tailplane and increased fuel capacity.

A Hastings pilot engaged in the Berlin Airlift recalled, 'The Hastings had its teething problems and, with its conventional type of undercarriage, had difficulty with a crosswind component when this was stronger than 20 knts. This compared unfavourably with the C-54 Skymaster, which had a tricycle

Below: A head-on shot of a Hastings C1. Note crew member in the astrodome.

Above: Hastings C1s were operated by No 99 Squadron at RAF Lyneham from September 1949, as part of the Transport Wing (including Nos 53 and 511 Squadrons).

undercarriage and was able to operate in considerably more severe conditions. The first Hastings squadron had been deployed to Germany well ahead of schedule, but this was justified by the high standards of flying under the exacting conditions of the Airlift.'

The Hastings was first delivered to an overseas station when No 70 Squadron re-equipped from Vickers Valettas in the Middle East in early 1956. The following year, the Far East Air Force also received Hastings when No 48 Squadron disposed of its Valettas at Changi. Hastings replaced Yorks in the long-range passenger-carrying role at Lyneham. During the Suez campaign of 1956 Hastings of No 70 Squadron, based in Cyprus, dropped paratroops into Port Said in Egypt.

When the larger, turboprop-powered Britannia was introduced in 1959, Hastings ceased to fly trunk routes and were deployed to tactical transport operations. They were withdrawn from front-line service in 1968, being replaced by Hercules and Argosies. Sixteen Hastings were converted for

weather reconnaissance duties and served at Gibraltar and Aldergrove until 1964. Another special version was the T5, with a large ventral radome of which eight were converted for use with the Bomber Command Bombing School at RAF Lindholme, for providing bomb-aimers with training in the use of basic electronic equipment.

POWERPLANT: Four 1249kW (1675hp) Bristol Hercules 106 sleeve-valve radial engines (C2)
SPAN: 34.44m (113ft 0in); Length: 25.19m (82ft 8in)
MAX SPEED: 561km/h (348mph)
ACCOMMODATION: Crew of five; room for 30 equipped paratroops or 50 troops
FIRST AIRCRAFT FLOWN: 7 May 1946
ENTERED SERVICE: September 1948 (C1, No 47 Squadron)
LAST RAF SERVICE: June 1977 (C2, No 230 OCU).

De HAVILLAND CANADA CHIPMUNK

After the war, the RAF had an urgent need to replace its Tiger Moths, particularly with the post-war Reserve Flying Schools and University Air Squadrons. Designed and developed by de Havilland Canada, the DHC1 Chipmunk that was first flown in May 1946 at Toronto, was successfully evaluated at Boscombe Down. It was adopted as an *ab initio* trainer, fully equipped to RAF requirements, with blind flying panels, radio and manually-operated variable-pitch propeller. A total of 740 were delivered to the RAF between 1950 and October 1953.

Eventually the Chipmunk became standard equipment with all seventeen University Air Squadrons and the eighteen Reserve Flying Schools of the RAFVR, until the latter were closed as an economy measure in 1952–53. Because of the expansion of the RAF, due to the Korean War, additional Chipmunk-equipped Basic Flying Training Schools were set up for the instruction of

Below: Initial deliveries of the Chipmunk to the RAF began in February 1950 and the first units to receive them were the University Air Squadrons. During the expansion of the RAF pilot training programme in 1951–52, the Chipmunk was chosen for the *ab initio* instruction of the National Service pilots.

1950

Left: From July 1965, the Chipmunk was re-introduced for the training of direct-entry pilots in the Primary Flying Squadron at South Cerney (later Church Fenton) as a preliminary to initial jet training on Jet Provosts on FTS.

National Service pilots. Four members of the Royal Family have flown solo on RAF Chipmunks.

From 1965, the Chipmunk was re-introduced for the training of direct-entry pilots in the Primary Flying Squadron as a preliminary to initial jet training on Jet Provosts. In spite of being replaced in the University Air Squadrons by the Bulldog, many remained in service with the Elementary Flying Training School at RAF Swinderby and, for even longer (until early 1996), at the twelve Air Experience Flights flying ATC cadets. At Gatow in Berlin, two Chipmunks served for thirty-eight years until 1994, exercising the British occupation forces' right to fly over the city.

Flight Lieutenant Peter Bouch who flew the Chipmunk with the Flying Selection Squadron at Swinderby recalls, 'It was robust, simple to operate, yet because of a tailwheel configuration quite demanding in its handling – particularly on or near the ground. It was a very basic, simple little machine, with nicely balanced controls, fully automatic, spinnable and ideal for the full RAF primary flying syllabus. It could operate equally well from grass or concrete, but being light made it vulnerable to strong and cross

winds, so we had to be careful with it. Having said that, it was the best aircraft for the job. It is a much loved old aeroplane, excellent for the task and outlasted many of its successors.'

POWERPLANT: One 108kW (145hp) de Havilland Gipsy Major 8 in-line piston engine
SPAN: 10.46m (34ft 4in); Length: 7.82m (25ft 8in)
MAX SPEED: 223km/h (138mph)
ACCOMMODATION: Two seats in tandem
FIRST AIRCRAFT FLOWN: 22 May 1946
ENTERED RAF SERVICE: February 1950 (Oxford UAS)
LAST RAF SERVICE: 31 March 1996.

AVRO SHACKLETON

Above: The 'Interim Solution' or 'Temporary Expedient' that lasted thirteen years. No 8 Squadron received twelve AEW2 Shackletons, fitted with an undernose radome from redundant FAA Fairey Gannets, for Airborne Early Warning duties. These remained operational until the introduction of the Boeing E.3 Sentry.

The value of the four-engined landplane in the long-range maritime role was proved by the use of Flying Fortresses and Liberators by Coastal Command during World War II. When these Lend-Lease aircraft were returned to the USA the RAF sought a development of the Avro Lincoln. This emerged as the Shackleton, a maritime reconnaissance version of the bomber. It retained the Lincoln's wings and undercarriage, but had a redesigned fuselage and Rolls-Royce Griffon engines with six-blade contra-rotating propellers.

Early MR1s had a short nose with chin radome, but the MR2 introduced a long streamlined nose and a new type of semi-retractable 'dustbin' radome aft of the wings. After five years in service, the MR3 was introduced which had a nosewheel undercarriage and featured wingtip tanks. To assist take-offs with heavier loads later models were fitted with two Bristol Siddeley Viper auxiliary turbojets in the outer engine nacelles.

Sergeant Signaller 'Dinty' More AFC remembers that the Shackleton with its large crew requirement engendered 'a great spirit'. He recalls, 'I look back on the Shackleton with great affection. It did not quite have the "aura" of a Lancaster, but it was much more comfortable than a Lincoln. It was noisy, it vibrated, it was draughty, it threw exhaust stubs, its heaters didn't work properly but in its day it was the best anti-submarine aircraft in the world. It had a rest bed, a galley, new radar sonics and you could actually walk around in it.'

With the arrival of the Nimrod MR1 in 1970, Shackletons were withdrawn from service with the maritime reconnaissance squadrons. But this was not

Above: The main differences which emerged in the Mk 3 design were the tricycle/ nosewheel undercarriage, wingtip fuel tanks and a 'wrap-around' clear vision pilots' cockpit screen. The ultimate Mk 3 Phase 3 had such an increase in weight that this version had to be assisted off the ground by a pair of jets.

the end of its RAF service. Following the demise of the RN's big aircraft carriers and with them the Fairey Gannet AEW3, the RAF assumed the role of providing airborne early warning aircraft to counter low-level intruders probing the UK air defence region. Twelve Shackleton MR2s were converted to AEW2 configuration, with a large radome under the nose. No 8 Squadron was re-formed in 1972 to operate the AEW2s until their replacement with the Nimrod AEW3. The service life of this 'stop-gap' aircraft was much longer than planned, after the cancellation of the AEW Nimrod programme. No 8 Squadron's Shackletons remained operational until the E-3D Sentry AEW1s service début in 1991.

POWERPLANT: Four 1827kW (2450hp) Rolls-Royce Griffon 57A in-line piston engines (MR2)
SPAN: 36.57m (120ft); Length: 26.59m (87ft 3in)
MAX SPEED: 484km/h (300mph)
TYPICAL ARMAMENT: Twin 20mm guns in nose; depth charges and/or bombs to a maximum of 6818kg (15,000lb) carried internally
FIRST AIRCRAFT FLOWN: 9 March 1949
ENTERED RAF SERVICE: April 1951 (MR1, No 120 Squadron)
LAST RAF SERVICE: July 1991 (AEW2, No 8 Squadron).

ENGLISH ELECTRIC CANBERRA

Below: The prototype English Electric Canberra, with Roland Beamont at the controls, during an early test flight in 1949. The top of the rudder has the modified shape introduced after the first flight.

The Canberra was the RAF's first jet bomber, built as a replacement for the DH Mosquito. Following the Korean War it became obvious that the RAF urgently needed a jet bomber, capable of holding its own with the new generation of fighters, until the V-bomber force became operational. Fortunately the unarmed Canberra bridged the gap.

Wing Commander Roland P Beamont, who made the first flight in the Canberra recalled, 'Friday, 13 May 1949 ushered in a new era in aviation – that of the high altitude jet bomber. The overriding impressions were of a straight forward and simple aeroplane with conventional stability and response to controls, exceptional smoothness and lack of high noise level from engine and aerodynamic sources. It

had that indefinable impression of engineering and aerodynamic integrity that all pilots recognize in the description "a pilot's aeroplane".'

During test flights the Canberra made the first out-and-back crossing of the Atlantic in one day by any aircraft. The unique design concept of a bomber/reconnaissance aircraft meant that the Canberra had a performance well in excess of current fighters. Operating from Cyprus, Canberra B2s carried out numerous raids on Egyptian military targets during the Anglo–French intervention at Suez

Below: Intended for use in the electronic countermeasures role, the Canberra T17 has the type's distinctive large hemispherical radome and four small blister radomes. This T17A was with No 360 Squadron.

Right: The longest serving Canberra is the PR9, which entered RAF service in January 1960, and remains operational with No 39 (PRU) Squadron at RAF Marham today.

in October 1956. Bomber Command's home-based Light Bomber Force (LBF) reached a peak of twenty-three squadrons by April 1955 and deployed some 350 aircraft. As the 'V-Force' built up, Canberras were gradually phased out from home-based squadrons and used increasingly to establish a tactical nuclear strike force, in the Near and Far East.

The PR3, PR7 and PR9 photo-reconnaissance versions have been particularly long-serving, the latter becoming the last variant to remain in front-line use with the RAF. PR9s have recently been employed over Bosnia on UN intelligence-gathering sorties.

Above: A glazed nose for the provision of visual bomb aiming, and a third seat for the bomb aimer, were fitted to the Canberra B2 – the first to enter service in May 1951.

The dual-control Canberra T4 trainer was introduced in 1952, sixty-eight being produced. Probably the least elegant variant of the classic bomber was the Canberra T17 with its extended nose, which served for nearly four decades providing aircrew with experience of modern electronic warfare techniques and the use of electronic countermeasures (ECM). These T17s were finally withdrawn in October 1994. The Canberra TT18 was a target-towing conversion of B2 bombers and served with No 100 Squadron until superseded by Hawks in January 1992.

POWERPLANT: Two 50.10kN (11,250lb st) Rolls-Royce Avon 206 turbojets (PR9)
SPAN: 20.67m (67ft 10in); Length: 20.31m (66ft 8in)
MAX SPEED: 903km/h (560mph)
TYPICAL ARMAMENT: Max bomb load 2727kg (6000lb) (B2)
FIRST AIRCRAFT FLOWN: 13 May 1949
ENTERED RAF SERVICE: May 1951 (B2, No 101 Squadron); PR7 and PR9 still current.

BRISTOL SYCAMORE

The Bristol Sycamore marked a milestone for the RAF, as the first British-designed helicopter to enter service. In 1949 thirteen were taken on charge by the Ministry of Supply for evaluation, and three went to RAF Coastal Command as HR12s. Fitted with a Westland hydraulic winch, over a sliding door, this was the first use of a helicopter by the RAF for search and rescue (SAR) work. With the adoption of the improved HR13/14 by the RAF, the Sycamore went into service in April 1953 with No 275 Squadron, the RAF's first dedicated SAR squadron, at Linton-on-Ouse.

In 1954 the Sycamore entered service in Malaya where it joined, and ultimately replaced, the Dragonfly. The Sycamore also served with No 284 Squadron in Cyprus during the EOKA problems, where it pioneered two important operating techniques – night flying and dropping troops in mountainous terrain. In 1958 five Sycamores successfully dropped forty-one troops near a terrorist hideout 3000ft up in the Troodos Mountains near Nicosia, Cyprus.

Flight Lieutenant Ian Taylor recalled an episode when a No 110 Squadron Sycamore went to find an Auster reconnaissance aircraft that had crashed in the Malayan jungle along the Thai border, 'The chances of finding an aircraft among the trees was remote; the chance of a pilot still being alive seemed even more remote. Then I heard a faint "bleep bleep" on my radio, which I recognized as the distinctive signal of the SARAH homing beacon carried by pilots. Thirteen men of the SAS were flown out to the scene of the crash and winched down by Sycamores to clear a landing site. The Auster pilot was Captain John Tadman of 656 Squadron AAC who had been engaged in Communist Terrorist patrols. One week later I landed the Sycamore and recovered Tadman on a stretcher and flew him to the British Military Hospital in Taiping, seventy miles away.'

From 1963, Sycamores operated in Borneo, but the helicopter was not really suitable for 'hot and high' conditions, and serviceability was a problem. They were withdrawn from front-line duties in October 1964. A small number of HC14s remained at RAF Northolt for passenger carrying duties purposes until August 1972.

Below: During the EOKA problems in Cyprus in the late 1950s, the Bristol Sycamore was used for troop movements on the Island. Here troops of the Gloucestershire Regiment are engaged in helicopter training from a Sycamore HR14.

POWERPLANT: One 410kW (550hp) Alvis Leonides 73 piston engine (HC14)
ROTOR DIAMETER: 14.80m (48ft 7in); Length: 14.06m (46ft 2in)
MAX SPEED: 204km/h (127mph)
ACCOMMODATION: Crew of two; could carry two stretchers or three passengers
FIRST AIRCRAFT FLOWN: 24 July 1947
ENTERED RAF SERVICE: 19 February 1952 (HR12)
LAST RAF SERVICE: August 1972 (HC14, No 32 Squadron).

HAWKER HUNTER

Right: In common with most single-seat fighters adopted by the RAF, the Hunter was adapted for dual-control training duties. This is a farewell flight of Hunter T7s from RAF Lossiemouth in September 1993, shortly before the Hunter was retired.

The Hunter was unquestionably one of Britain's most successful post-war military aircraft, a true thoroughbred and arguably the most graceful fighter of the era. Although Sir Sydney Camm's design underwent a number of modifications, including wing extensions, a larger engine and the addition of an airbrake – the basic shape was 'right' from the outset.

The relatively short range of the Hunter F1 and F2 was extended in the subsequent F4 with additional fuel in the wings, while more underwing stores could now be carried. North Weald-based No 111 Squadron received the F4 in 1955, and a year later Hunters were operational in strength in Germany. Fitted with the more powerful Avon 203 engine, the Hunter F6 had equipped all of the RAF's day fighter squadrons in Europe by 1958.

Rod Dean, who had twenty years and nearly 3000 hours of association with the Hunter in the RAF recalls, 'I was sitting on the runway at RAF Chivenor, home of RAF fighter pilots, in Hunter F6 XG131 on 25 November 1964, for my first solo. The Hunter groundschool, four hours in the Hunter "box" and four dual in the T7 had prepared me for this moment – my first ever flight in a single-seat Hunter. There was no preparation for the noise of 10,000lb of thrust, the view (the T7 was fairly claustrophobic) and the

Below: The last Hunter being used by an RAF Unit. This F6A was still being operated in 1998 by DERA at Llanbedr.

1953

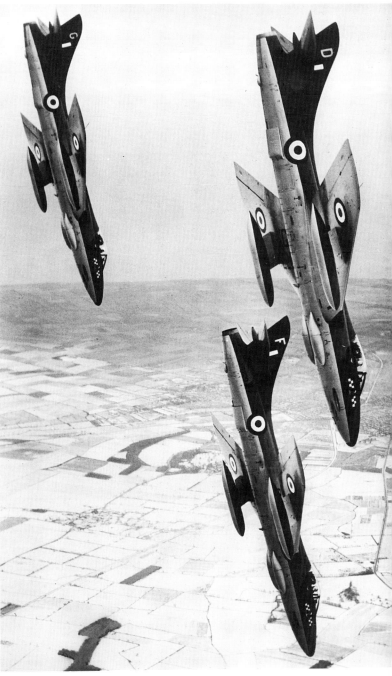

Left: After retirement from front-line service Hunter FGADs were used for operational conversion at RAF Clivenor and Brawdy.

Above: Three Hawker Hunter F6 of No 92 Squadron based at RAF Middleton St George performing aerobatics over the snow-covered East Coast in the late 1950s.

Above: The Hawker Hunter F6 was built in larger numbers than any other Hunter, a total of 383 being supplied to the RAF.

sheer exhilaration of being airborne in one of the best British fighters ever. The low-speed handling was impeccable, with plenty of warning before anything unusual happened.'

After the Lightning had replaced it as the RAF's primary day fighter, Hunters remained in service with an improved ground-attack capability. The FGA9 was used both at home, pending the delivery of Harrier GR1s, and in the Middle and Far East. A two-seat operational trainer, the Hunter T7 was the last version to enter service, in 1958, and was widely used by Operational Conversion/Tactical Weapons Units and Flying Training Schools prior to the Hawk's arrival. The last Hunters (T7s) were retired in 1994 at RAF Lossiemouth, after use by the Buccaneer squadrons.

POWERPLANT: One 44.53kN (1000lb st) Rolls-Royce Avon 203 turbojet
Span: 10.26m (33ft 8in); Length: 13.98m (45ft 10.5in)
MAX SPEED: 1144km/h (710mph)
TYPICAL ARMAMENT: Four 30mm Aden cannon; underwing pylons for two 454kg (1000lb) bombs and twenty-four 76.2mm (3in) rockets
FIRST AIRCRAFT FLOWN: 20 June 1951 (P1067); 16 May 1953 (Hunter F1)
ENTERED RAF SERVICE: July 1954 (F1, No 43 Squadron)
LAST RAF SERVICE: April 1994 (T7, No 208 Squadron).

WESTLAND WHIRLWIND

Above: RAF Whirlwind 10s were successfully used as a military transport in support of the army, especially as seen here in Borneo in 1964.

Soon after the Dragonfly had entered service, Westland announced that licence agreements had been finalized in November 1950 with Sikorsky for construction of the Sikorsky S-55 for the British forces. Named the Whirlwind, it was immediately popular with its maintenance crews as its engine, mounted in the nose instead of above the cabin, was readily accessible for inspections by opening two hinged doors.

The first variant for the RAF was the HAR2 that entered service with Coastal Command's search and rescue organisation in which role the yellow-painted Whirlwind became a familiar sight around the coast of the UK. The HAR4, equipped for operations in tropical climates, was used for jungle rescue and transport work in Malaya, becoming the RAF's first genuine troop-carrying helicopter. These piston-engined Whirlwinds were subsequently replaced by a turbine-powered version, the Mk10.

In 1959, two Whirlwind HCC8s were specially

Above: Powered by a Bristol Siddeley Gnome turbo-shaft the Whirlwind HAR10 was used for search and rescue, both in the UK and overseas.

equipped for duties with the Queen's Flight, having four seats in the cabin with special furnishings and soundproofing. Five years later, a further pair of turbine-powered HCC12s were added to the Queen's Flight and they served until December 1967, when replaced by the Wessex. Harald Penrose, former Chief Test Pilot at Westland recalls the first flight of a Whirlwind to Buckingham Palace, 'The advantage of helicoptering had so appealed to the Duke of Edinburgh that he decided to add a Whirlwind to the Queen's Flight and learn how to pilot it so that he could fly directly from the Palace on his many engagements. Having donned our neatest suits, test pilot Roy Bradley and I set out from Yeovil, heading for London. Later we encircle the Palace grounds, which to my surprise were big enough to land an Auster. With smooth precision Roy brought the Whirlwind down, hovered at the foot of the wide stone stairs leading from the Palace to the garden and lightly touched down on the lawn and cut the engine. Nobody was to be seen, "What do we do now?", Roy inquires. Actually Her Majesty had gone to Balmoral,

that's why we did it that day. One landing and take-off was all that was needed. More practically, that flight led to fuller consideration of using London's empty South Bank site adjacent to Waterloo Bridge as a heliport.'

POWERPLANT: One 4.67kN (1050shp) Bristol Siddeley Gnome H1000 turbine (HAR/HC10)
ROTOR DIAMETER: 16.15m (53ft); Fuselage length: 19.09m (62ft 4in)
MAX SPEED: 177km/h (110mph)
ACCOMMODATION: Crew of three with space for eight passengers
FIRST AIRCRAFT FLOWN: 15 August 1953 (RN HAR1)
ENTERED RAF SERVICE: February 1955 (HAR2, No 22 Squadron)
LAST RAF SERVICE: November 1981 (HAR10, No 202 Squadron).

BLACKBURN BEVERLEY

Below: A high-wing layout was adopted for the Blackburn Beverley to facilitate rapid cargo loading and give maximum head-room in the freight hold. This is an early production model.

Good looks, plus an ability to carry bulky and heavy loads in and out of short fields, seldom go hand in hand, and the Beverley was no exception. Originally designed by General Aircraft, it was a simple unpressurized aircraft with fixed landing gear. New techniques in parachuting stores demanded large rear-loading doors and the tailboom provided passenger accommodation. Though limited in speed and range, the Beverley nicknamed 'Barrack Block' and 'Pregnant Portia' could accommodate a wide range of military equipment and a complement of thirty-six passengers. It was at the time the largest aircraft to be delivered to the RAF.

A Beverley pilot recalled his time with No 47 Squadron at RAF Abingdon, 'Greeted at first by RAF aircrews with some dismay as an ugly monster, the 'Bev' quickly earned our affection by its robust reliability when operating in challenging terrain such as desert landing strips and its endless adaptability to carry heavy loads of all descriptions. There was a short period when Beverleys were grounded following a spate of engine fires in the air, but this was rectified by introducing a later variant of the Centaurus engine which proved to be trouble-free, and they went on to earn great laurels.'

The vast fuselage provided a main cabin or cargo hold and tests with para-dropping loads culminated in

the drop of an 18,144kg (40,000lb) load beneath eight parachutes. As a transport it could carry ninety-four troops or seventy fully equipped paratroops. The type served eventually with five squadrons in widely separated parts of the world including Africa, Brunei, the Middle East and Singapore as well as in the UK. Beverleys also flew supplies to British forces in the Yemen in 1957, and operated during the Kuwait crisis and the Kenyan relief operations of 1961. When based at Khormaksar they were active in the Radfan campaigns. Final retirement came in 1968, when the first of sixty-six turboprop Lockheed C-130K Hercules came into service.

Below: The dropping of heavy loads by parachute was an essential design demand for the Beverley, and was the first British designed transport to incorporate this. Here a Beverley of No 47 Squadron at RAF Abingdon is supply dropping over Weston-on-the-Green in September 1961.

POWERPLANT: Four 2125kW (2850hp) Bristol Centaurus 273 sleeve-valve radial piston engines
SPAN: 49.37m (162ft 0in); Length: 30.30m (99ft 5in)
MAX SPEED: 383km/h (238mph)
ACCOMMODATION: Crew of four; max payload 45,000lb of freight, or 94 troops or 70 fully-equipped paratroops
FIRST AIRCRAFT FLOWN: 20 June 1950 (GAL60 Universal)
ENTERED RAF SERVICE: March 1956 (No 47 Squadron)
LAST RAF SERVICE: 6 December 1968.

VICKERS VALIANT

Above: The Valiant was the first of the V-bombers capable of accommodating the Blue Steel stand-off weapon. The first squadron to receive Valiants was No 138 at RAF Gaydon, in 1955, thus creating the nucleus of Britain's deterrent force of fast, high-altitude bombers carrying nuclear weapons over great distances with accurate delivery.

With the use of nuclear weapons over Japan in August 1945, the RAF realized that a new generation of long-range, jet-powered bomber aircraft would be required, if the nation was to maintain its leading edge in the coming years. This operational requirement produced three successful designs from Vickers, Avro and Handley Page for the RAF's V-bomber force, of which the Vickers Valiant was the first to enter operational service in 1955.

The Valiant had a high-set wing incorporating compound sweep, a pressurized cabin for its five-man crew and was powered by four Rolls-Royce Avon turbojets. It was used operationally to deploy high-explosive bombs during the Suez Campaign of October 1956, and also dropped the UK's first atomic bomb over Maralinga, South Australia that same month in the course of Operation *Buffalo*. Another Valiant B1 released the first British thermonuclear

weapon over the Pacific Ocean at Christmas Island as part of Operation *Grapple* in May 1957.

The development of Soviet surface-to-air anti-aircraft missiles resulted in a change of tactics for the V-force from its high-altitude strategic bombing role to low-level penetration of enemy airspace. Designed for the less demanding environment, from a structural point of view, above 40,000ft, rather than the turbulent buffeting below 500ft, the Valiant was soon in difficulties. Tests showed that constant low-level operations were causing serious wing spar metal fatigue. Although some aircraft were employed as tankers, the whole fleet had been prematurely withdrawn from service by January 1965, leaving the Vulcan and Victor to soldier on.

Four variants of the 104 Valiants produced, flew with ten squadrons, during their nine-year career with Bomber Command. The B(PR)1 had a dual capability as a long-range strategic photo-reconnaissance aircraft. The tanker variants pioneered day and night in-flight refuelling in the RAF, thereby extending the operational range and flexibility of both the V-force and front-line fighters such as the Javelin and Lightning.

Below: Being less advanced aerodynamically than the Vulcan and Victor, the Vickers Valiant could be available at an earlier date – which was an attraction for the Air Ministry when the V-bombers were contemplated.

Right: Early in 1959 No 214 Squadron, based at RAF Marham, started a series of operational trials of the flight-refuelling system using the Valiant. This proved satisfactory and gave the V-bomber force greater flexibility and radius of action and fortified its strategic dispositions.

POWERPLANT: Four 44.76kN (10,050lb st) Rolls-Royce RA28 Avon 204/205 turbojets
SPAN: 34.85m (114ft 4in); Length: 32.99m (108ft 3in)
MAX SPEED: 912km/h (567mph)
TYPICAL ARMAMENT: No defensive weapons. Conventional or nuclear weapons carried internally, to max bomb load of 9525kg (21,000lb)
FIRST AIRCRAFT FLOWN: 18 May 1951
ENTERED RAF SERVICE: February 1955 (B1, No 138 Squadron)
LAST RAF SERVICE: February 1965 (BK1, No 214 Squadron).

AVRO VULCAN

Right: The advent of the powerful Olympus engines made possible the much more advanced Vulcan B2 with increased span and used as a launching platform for the Blue Steel 'stand-off' bomb, as carried to this Vulcan of No 27 Squadron based at Scampton in 1961.

Below: Together with the Victor, the Vulcan B2s provided the UK's Nuclear Deterrent until the role was taken over by Royal Navy submarines equipped with Polaris missiles in 1967. Here is a line-up of Vulcan B2s at a Quick Reaction Alert (QRA) location.

First flown in 1952, the Vulcan, designed by Roy Chadwick, was the world's first delta-wing heavy bomber. The Vulcan, nicknamed 'Aluminium Overcast', was a bold design, which in service ably met the RAF's changing operational requirements for nearly thirty years. Forming a key part of Britain's nuclear deterrent through much of the Cold War, four Vulcans were kept at immediate readiness to be airborne in two minutes from the start of the engines, at each of the operational bases. The improved Vulcan B2 entered service in 1960, and was to have been equipped with the Skybolt missile. When development of this was halted in 1963, Blue Steel was planned as the primary weapon. By 1970, with the adoption of the submarine-launched Polaris missile as the nation's major deterrent weapon, the Vulcan was adapted for a long-range, low-level attack role equipped with advanced ECM and a range of conventional and nuclear tactical weapons.

With replacement by the Tornado GR1 imminent, the Vulcan force was due to disband in 1982 – however, as is now legendary, the Falklands War halted these plans. The extraordinary Black Buck operations on ultra long-range strikes on the Falklands, refuelled by Victor tankers from Ascension

Above: Few aircraft have ever created such an impression as the Avro Vulcan. This almost perfect delta triangle had fighter-like manoeuvrability. The wing was some seven feet thick at the roof end enabling drag to be kept to a minimum by enclosing engines, undercarriage, fuel and bomb-load entirely within it.

Island, gave the bomber its first actual taste of combat. Squadron Leader C N McDougall, pilot of Vulcan XM597 engaged on Black Buck 6 recorded, 'We were launched from Wideawake late on 2 June, this time armed with four Shrikes for another strike against the Falklands radar. We commenced the final run-in during the early hours of 3 June and some forty minutes were spent waiting overhead for the radar to be switched on. The aircraft's RWR picked up an Ejercito Skyguard radar and two Shrikes were launched, destroying the radar which had been acting as a fire control unit for one of the GADA 601 anti-aircraft batteries close to Port Stanley. Due to a critical fuel state we were forced to leave the area and assisted by a Nimrod MR2 we made a successful rendezvous with our Victor tanker about half-way back to Wideawake. However, the tip of the Vulcan's refuelling probe broke off during the AAR and we were forced to divert to the nearest airfield – Rio de Janeiro in Brazil.'

During the Falklands conflict six Vulcans were converted as air refuelling tankers and were flown by No 50 Squadron – the last RAF unit to operate the Vulcan when these K2s were withdrawn in March 1984.

Overleaf: The last Vulcan B2 squadron, No 44, was disbanded in December 1982. A Vulcan Display Flight, equipped with XH558, and based at RAF Waddington enabled the majestic delta to continue thrilling crowds at summer airshows throughout the eighties and early nineties.

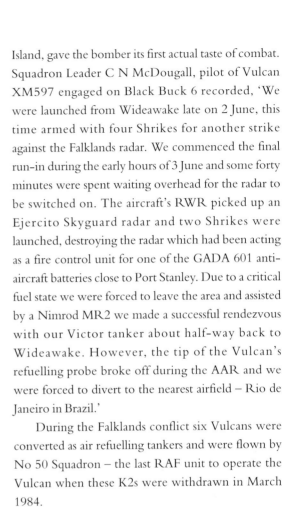

POWERPLANT: Four 89.06kN (20,000lb) Rolls-Royce Olympus 301 turbojets (B2)
SPAN: 33.83m (111ft 0in); Length: 30.45m (95ft 11in)
MAX SPEED: 1038km/h (645mph)
TYPICAL ARMAMENT: Up to twenty-one 454kg (1000lb) bombs carried internally
FIRST AIRCRAFT FLOWN: 30 August 1952
ENTERED RAF SERVICE: 20 July 1956 (B1, No 230 OCU)
LAST RAF SERVICE: 31 March 1984 (K2, No 50 Squadron).

De HAVILLAND COMET

The DH106 Comet 2, modified for service with the RAF, pioneered the use of the pure jet for military transport duties. Following crashes of early civilian Comets, caused by structural failure of the pressure cabin, Comet 2s being built for BOAC were modified for RAF service after the airline decided not to receive them. With the type's problems ironed out, Transport Command took delivery of fifteen Comet C2s from 1956, while two were used as crew trainers. Three of the C2s were fitted with specialized equipment and served with No 90 Group's two squadrons in the highly secret electronic intelligence (ELINT) gathering role.

No 216 Squadron, at RAF Lyneham, the world's first military jet transport squadron, established an impressive record with its Comets. The first operational flight was made on 23 June 1956 when XK670 flew the Air Minister to Moscow for the Soviet Air Force Day. Comets flew emergency services to Malta and Cyprus during the Suez crisis and regular sorties to Australia and Christmas Island in the Pacific. These jet transports brought the most distant parts of the Commonwealth to within less than two days travelling time of the UK, and the Far East inside twenty-four hours.

Below: Five Comet C4s were delivered to No 216 Squadron at RAF Lyneham in 1962. This could be distinguished by its longer fuselage and wing tanks. The maximum speed was raised with higher power turbojets.

173

Above: The de Havilland Comet Series 2, modified for service with the RAF, pioneered the use of the pure jet for military transport duties. RAF Transport Command took delivery of fifteen early Comets and these served with No 216 Squadron at RAF Lyneham – the world's first military jet transport squadron.

The Comet 4C was the final production version, combining the stretched fuselage of the Comet 4B with the wings of the Comet 4. Five Comet C4s were delivered to No 216 Squadron and had ninety-four rear facing seats, easily convertible for ambulance duties to carry twelve stretchers, forty-seven sitting cases and six attendants. They could be distinguished by their longer fuselages and external long-range wing tanks. In April 1967 the Comet C2s were withdrawn from Transport Command and after defence cuts the five Comet C4s were retired from service at Lyneham shortly before No 216 Squadron disbanded on 30 June 1975.

POWERPLANT: Four 32.8kN (7350lb st) Rolls-Royce Avon 117/118 turbojets (Comet C2)
SPAN: 35.05m (115ft 0in); Length: 29.26m (96ft 0in)
MAX SPEED: 790km/h (490mph)
ACCOMMODATION: Crew of five and forty-four passengers
FIRST AIRCRAFT FLOWN: 27 July 1949 (Comet 1)
ENTERED RAF SERVICE: 7 July 1956 (T2, No 216 Squadron)
LAST RAF SERVICE: June 1975 (C4, No 216 Squadron).

GLOSTER JAVELIN

Below: The Gloster Javelin was the first aircraft designed in Britain explicitly as a night and all-weather fighter. It was on a most generous scale with a vast delta wing.

The Gloster Javelin was the first delta-wing fighter aircraft to be operated by the RAF. It was an advanced machine, and the service's first all-weather fighter to be designed as such from the outset, entering service with No 46 Squadron in February 1956. With its lightly-loaded large-area delta wing it had an excellent high-altitude performance. Its design incorporated a T-tail with all swept surfaces which, in conjunction with wing trailing edge flaps, allowed landings to be made without an excessively nose-high altitude.

The crew of two were seated in tandem, in pressurized accommodation, and an airborne interception radar was installed in the nose. It had a broad and flattened fuselage, with two Bristol Siddeley Sapphire engines. Forty Javelin FAW1s were delivered and served in Germany from August 1957. The FAW2 had American radar, thirty of this version being built, while the FAW4 was the first to embody an all-moving tailplane. Subsequent models had additional fuel tankage in the wings.

Major changes were introduced to the FAW7, with more powerful Sapphire 7 engines, and this was the first variant to carry Firestreak infrared air-to-air

Above: The FAW8 was the final production version of the Javelin and the first to be powered by the Sapphire Sa76 which had limited reheat. AI22 radar was carried and the standard armament was four Firestreak air-to-air missiles on underwing pylons.

missiles as standard armament. In 1960, four Javelins, using in-flight refuelling, made the first non-stop flight from the UK to Singapore.

Twenty-one two-seat dual-control T3 trainer versions were built for Fighter Command's Javelin conversion unit, No 228 OCU. Production of the Javelin for the RAF reached 427 of all marks, and at peak strength the inventory totalled fourteen squadrons. Javelins also served in Cyprus, Zambia and Singapore, and the type played an important role in fighter operations during the Indonesian Confrontation between 1962–66. The last operational squadron in the European theatre was No 11 Squadron in Germany which flew Javelins until January 1966.

POWERPLANT: Two 48.98kN (11,000lb st) Bristol Siddeley Sapphire turbojets with reheat (FAW9)
SPAN: 15.85m (52ft 0in); Length: 17.15m (56ft 3in)
MAX SPEED: 1141km/h (709mph)
TYPICAL ARMAMENT: Two 30mm Aden guns in the wings and four de Havilland Firestreak AAMs or four packs each with thirty-seven 2in unguided air-to-air rockets
FIRST AIRCRAFT FLOWN: 26 November 1951
ENTERED RAF SERVICE: February 1956 (FAW1, No 46 Squadron)
LAST RAF SERVICE: April 1968 (FAW9, No 60 Squadron).

HANDLEY PAGE VICTOR

Below: The Victor's outstanding versatility bestowed upon it the longest service of all the V-bomber generation, and the tanker version bowed out in 1993.

The Handley Page Victor was the last of the V-bombers to enter service with the RAF. Technically highly advanced for its time, the Victor was designed to operate fast and high, above virtually all known defences. A crescent shaped wing was chosen to allow the highest cruising speeds, the four engines being buried in the sharply swept wing roots. Soon after it entered service, Soviet fighters and missiles were introduced which were capable of interception at its designed operating altitudes.

The Victor B2 flew in February 1959 and was larger, heavier and more powerful. Armament was the Blue Steel stand-off bomb which became operational in 1964. It became vulnerable at heights of over 50,000ft, and the aircraft's role was changed to include low-level attack. The SR2 was a strategic reconnaissance version, with the primary role of high-altitude maritime reconnaissance. A single Victor could radar-map the entire Mediterranean in a seven-hour sortie.

In 1965, with the demise of the Valiant, the Victor came into service as its replacement in the RAF's in-flight refuelling force. The K2 had its wing span reduced to 34.4m (113ft) to help extend the fatigue life of the reconditioned airframes. During the Falklands conflict, Victor K2s made an outstanding contribution to the success of the campaign, tanking the Black Buck Vulcans and other aircraft over the South Atlantic. Their final call came in the Gulf campaign in 1991 prior to being retired at the end of 1993.

Right: To achieve the highest cruising Mach number the wing of the Handley Page Victor was designed to what is called a 'crescent' shape.

Wing Commander (now Group Captain) David Williams, then Officer Commanding of No 55 Squadron at RAF Marham engaged in Operation *Desert Storm* recalls their tanking missions, 'On 19 January 1991, an additional Victor was sent to supplement the other six, as up to a maximum of fourteen refuelling sorties were being flown per day. Many sorties were flown over the Persian Gulf in

Above: Two squadrons of Victor tankers were formed Nos 55 and 57, both at RAF Marham. No 57 disbanded in April 1986, but No 55 was still at work with the RAF's in-flight refuelling service until 1993.

1957

POWERPLANT: Four 89.06kN (20,600lb st) Rolls-
Royce Conway Mk 201 turbofans (B2)
SPAN: 36.48m (120ft 0in); Length: 35.03m (114ft
11in)
MAX SPEED: 1030km/h (640mph)
TYPICAL ARMAMENT: Various nuclear or
conventional weapons, including up to thirty-five
454kg (1000lb) bombs or one Blue Steel Mk 1 air-to-
surface missile semi-recessed beneath fuselage
FIRST AIRCRAFT FLOWN: 24 December 1952
ENTERED RAF SERVICE: 28 November 1957 (B1, No
232 OCU)
LAST RAF SERVICE: 15 October 1993 (K2, No 55
Squadron).

support of attack missions and air defence patrols and
together with 138 Olive Trails and numerous other
combat air patrols, 299 sorties were flown over the
forty-two day war at an average of thirty-three
missions per crew. The Victor detachment achieved
every objective and did not fall down on any
operational sortie.'

Left: The Victor's outstanding
versatility bestowed upon it the
longest service of all the V-bomber
generation.

BRISTOL BRITANNIA

Twenty-three Britannias were completed by Short Brothers and Harland at Belfast for the RAF – twenty C1s were ordered directly for the RAF and three C2s that were frustrated civil sales that were taken on by the government. For their long-range strategic transport role they had a large forward freight door and could be fitted with rear-facing passenger seats.

In service, the Britannia was operated by two squadrons, Nos 99 and 511 at RAF Lyneham, and was a replacement for the Hastings. Its début in March 1959 provided Transport Command with its first turboprop transport aircraft, from which it was popularly named the 'Whispering Giant'. Following the introduction of central servicing arrangements the Britannias were pooled, in a similar way to a civilian airline, being operated jointly by crews of both squadrons.

An RAF pilot said of the 'Whispering Giant', 'I was initially suspicious of an aeroplane in which "the pilot isn't connected to the controls and the propellers aren't connected to the engines and everything else is done by electricity", but I had genuine regret at parting with the Britannia, which can be summed up as the most "kindly" aircraft I had ever flown.'

Following a devastating hurricane in British Honduras a Britannia, piloted by No 511 Squadron's commanding officer, established a record by flying evacuated British families from Palisadoes Airport,

Belize to RAF St Mawgan – a distance of 6695km (4160 miles) in 12hr 40m. This stands as the longest non-stop flight ever made by an RAF Britannia.

With major reductions in defence spending the Britannia was phased out of RAF service, and Nos 99 and 511 Squadrons were disbanded in January 1976.

POWERPLANT: Four 3072kW (4120ehp) Bristol Proteus 755 turboprops
SPAN: 43.36m (142ft 3in); **Length:** 37.87m (124ft 3in)
MAX SPEED: 639km/h (397mph)
ACCOMMODATION: Crew of five; could carry 113 troops, 53 stretcher cases or 37,400lb of freight
FIRST AIRCRAFT FLOWN: 16 August 1952
ENTERED RAF SERVICE: March 1959 (No 99 Squadron)
LAST RAF SERVICE: January 1976 (Nos 99 and 511 Squadrons).

Right: The military version of the Bristol Britannia civil airliner provided RAF Transport Command with a turboprop for strategic operations. This example, named *Argo*, was the second handed over to No 99 Squadron at RAF Lyneham in June 1959. All Britannias were given the name of stars.

Right: The Bristol Britannia operated widely on long-range strategic missions in many parts of the world, forming the basis for the rapid deployment of the Army's United Kingdom Strategic Reserve. This Britannia C2 *Acrux* carries the title Royal Air Force Support Command – the successor to RAF Transport Command.

ENGLISH ELECTRIC LIGHTNING

When the Lightning F1 entered squadron service in 1960 it heralded a new era for the RAF. W E 'Teddy' Petter, father of the Canberra was the prime mover behind the project for a supersonic research aircraft, the English Electric P1A. Re-engined with Rolls-Royce Avons as the P1B, the design eventually became the Lightning. The RAF then had a supersonic, all-weather interceptor carrying heat-seeking air-to-air guided missiles for the first time. Fighter Command had never seen such a spectacular advance in performance when the Lightning F1, capable of over twice the Hunter's maximum speed, entered service with No 74 Squadron at RAF Coltishall

Another step forward was the integration of the aircraft's missiles into a co-ordinated system with the Ferranti radar facilitating easier 'locking-on' to targets. More powerful Rolls-Royce Avons and provision to carry Red Top missiles produced the Lightning F3, these advances further improving the already impressive design though still it had not reached its full potential.

With longer range, an improved wing design and in-flight refuelling capability, the Lightning F6,

POWERPLANT: Two 69.82kN (15,680lb st) Rolls-Royce Avon 302 afterburning turbojets (F6)
SPAN: 10.61m (34ft 10in); Length: 16.84m (55ft 3in)
MAX SPEED: 2415km/h (1500mph)
TYPICAL ARMAMENT: Two 30mm Aden guns in ventral fairing. Firestreak or Red Top air-to-air missiles, or forty-four 50.4mm (2in) spin-stabilized rockets
FIRST AIRCRAFT FLOWN: 4 August 1954 (P1A)
ENTERED RAF SERVICE: December 1959 (Lightning F1, CFE)
LAST RAF SERVICE: June 1988 (F6, No 11 Squadron).

accompanied in the inventory by some F3s and two-seat T5s was a very capable interceptor until the end of its operational life. The Lightning is remembered with affection by most of its former pilots, not least because it was the last single-seat fighter on strength, without the 'unwelcome intrusion', of a second crewman! Replacement by the two-seat Phantom had begun in the 1970s, but Nos 5 and 11 Squadrons at RAF Binbrook remained operational on the Lightning until 1987 and 1988 respectively.

It was at Binbrook in 1987 that the last display of Lightnings 'en masse' delighted an airshow audience after many years of spectacular flying displays. One display pilot recalled his sequence, 'I started the acceleration for the display, but left the reheat until the airfield boundary. Easing down to 250ft, trimming load free at 550kts and lined up with the display axis. Reheat in and wait for the light-up – both lit – good! Reef into a 90° bank turn, away from the crowd, to let them hear the roar of the burners and then cancel – airbrakes out to kill the speed and tighten the turn. Hold 6° until 420kts, then airbrakes in, play the g against speed to arrive pointing at the crowd centre at 380kts. Pull up to the vertical–reheat lit and quarter roll onto display axis – keep pulling to complete the loop ... I looked over my shoulder to see the airfield and reflect on how lucky I am to be paid to do the job.'

Left: Fitted with overwing fuel tanks and a flight-refuelling probe, a Lightning F6 taking off for its retirement flight from the BAe airfield at Warton.

HUNTING JET PROVOST

Royal Air Force use of the piston-engined Provost T1 and jet-powered Vampire T11 in its training sequence seemed illogical to Hunting, who proceeded with the private-venture design of a turbojet-powered version of the Provost to provide a pupil with all-through jet training. Keeping the original wings and tail of the Provost it introduced a new fuselage housing the single turbine engine, retractable tricycle undercarriage and retained side-by-side seating.

Ten Jet Provost T1s were delivered to evaluate primary jet training techniques during 1955. Comparative trials took place at No 2 FTS,

Hullavington with two courses of students – one on piston-engined Provosts and the other on Jet Provosts. Apart from the introduction of the turbojet engine, the 'JP' for the first time introduced pilots to the nosewheel undercarriage at the start of their flying programme, a feature that has become universal on

Below: Jet Provost T3A from RAF Church Fenton based No 7 FTS in 1990.

Right: With easy handling qualities, the Jet Provost T5 was well suited to formation aerobatics and equipped several teams including the *Poachers* from RAF College Cranwell.

Above: Silhouetted against the setting sun, two Jet Provost T5s of the *Gemini Pair* from No 1 FTS perform a minor formation.

Previous page: A pair of Jet Provost T3As on a formation training exercise from No 1 Flying Training School at RAF Linton-on-Ouse.

front-line aircraft.

In 1957 it was decided that the Jet Provost would be standardized throughout Flying Training Command with an improved version, the T3. This had a more powerful engine, shortened undercarriage legs, wing-tip tanks, modified canopy and ejection seats. It was also the first RAF trainer to have UHF instead of VHF radio. Four years later the T4 entered service with the Flying Training Schools. Notable aerobatic teams flying the 'JP' included the *Macaws*, the *Lincolnshire Poachers*, the CFS *Red Pelicans* and the *Vipers*. The T5, introduced in 1969, had a pressurized cockpit and a redesigned hood of a more bulbous shape. Many T3s and T5s were subsequently upgraded with newer avionics and continued in service until replaced by Tucanos by the end of 1993.

Squadron Leader Allan Corkett was involved with the introduction into service of the Jet Provost at No 2 FTS and said, 'The world's first *ab initio* training

POWERPLANT: One 11.13kN (2500lb st) Bristol Siddeley Viper Mk 202 turbojet (T5A)
SPAN: 10.77m (35ft 4in); Length: 10.36m (34ft 0in)
MAX SPEED: 708km/h (440mph)
ACCOMMODATION: Dual side-by-side seating
FIRST AIRCRAFT FLOWN: 16 June 1954
ENTERED RAF SERVICE: August 1955 (T1, No 2 FTS)
LAST RAF SERVICE: 1993 (T5, No 6 FTS).

experiment was carried out at RAF Hullavington. The JP was a most pleasant aircraft to fly, with no handling problems. Its very small Viper engine was first rate. The training experiment proved a complete success, and the production mark JP, with its ejector seats and refinements which emanated from these trials, proved this over the following thirty years.'

ARMSTRONG WHITWORTH ARGOSY

Above: An Argosy of No 267 Squadron at RAF Benson demonstrating a tactical assault with a Wessex HC2 delivering a field gun.

The Argosy C1 was developed as a medium-range military freighter by Armstrong Whitworth to replace the Vickers Valetta. With a twin-boom configuration and powered by four Rolls-Royce Dart turboprops that had a characteristic high-pitched whine, it was popularly known throughout it RAF service as the 'Whistling Wheelbarrow'. A batch of fifty-six was built for the RAF, designated Argosy C1 – the new aircraft was able to operate both on tactical transport and for medium-range airlift missions.

A high-winged design, it incorporated a truncated fuselage with a rear ramp. Considerable design and development time was saved by using the Avro Shackleton wing. The hydraulically operated rear doors hinged upwards and downwards, as 'crocodile jaws' and were capable of being opened for the air-dropping of supplies and facilitated ground loading. A robust undercarriage allowed it to operate from semi-prepared strips and it was capable of short take-off and landing-runs.

Argosies equipped both the Middle East and Far East Forces and played an important part in the operations in Borneo during the confrontation with Indonesia. It was a popular aircraft, especially with paratroops. During the Rhodesian emergency in 1965 Argosies supported the Javelin contingent. But with the rapidly diminishing RAF commitment in overseas theatres in the late 1960s, the Argosy fleet became an early victim of retrenchment. Some were

Above: Operational with RAF Transport Command from February 1962, the Argosy C1 was used for medium-range and tactical transport duties until replaced by the Hercules in 1971.

subsequently converted and retained by the RAF for radar calibration duties.

An RAF pilot recalled the Argosy with affection, 'In over a decade of service with the RAF, the Argosy established for itself a reputation for versatility and reliability; its relatively simple systems and engineering and the notable reliability of the Dart engine, made it easy to maintain. It also became popular with the aircrews and with passengers, especially those who jumped from it, who much preferred it for this purpose to the aircraft which took its place in Air Support Command.'

POWERPLANT: Four 1097kW (2470eshp) Rolls-Royce Dart 101 turboprops
SPAN: 35.05m (115ft 0in); Length: 26.44m (86ft 9in)
MAX SPEED: 407km/h (253mph)
ACCOMMODATION: Crew of four; could carry 69 troops, 54 equipped paratroops, 48 stretchers or 13,182kg (29,000lb) of freight
FIRST AIRCRAFT FLOWN: December 1958 (AW650)
ENTERED RAF SERVICE: November 1961 (C1)
LAST RAF SERVICE: January 1978 (E1, No 115 Squadron).

HAWKER SIDDELEY GNAT

The Gnat was one of the most widely-known of the RAF's jet trainers, as a result of its outstanding performances in the hands of the *Red Arrows* display team before being replaced with the Hawk. The diminutive Gnat was originally designed by Folland Aircraft as a lightweight fighter to replace the RAF's Venoms in the ground attack role, but the Hunter was selected. However, the RAF did have a requirement for an unarmed, two-seat advanced trainer to replace the Vampire T11, and to follow the Jet Provost sections of the all-through jet training programme. In theory it had a simplified structure, designed so that comparatively major components could be easily replaced – but in practice, RAF ground crews took a less than complimentary view because of its small size and access.

In 1959 Folland was taken over by Hawker Siddeley and eventually contracts for ninety-one Gnats were awarded. The Central Flying School first introduced the type in 1962, but the major operator was No 4 FTS at Valley. In 1964 a formation aerobatic team, operating five yellow-painted Gnats, and known as the *Yellowjacks*, gave its first displays. The following year the team and its aircraft reformed as the *Red Arrows* at the Central Flying School.

In service the Gnat had its faults. It was not particularly stable but had sensitive controls that made it very manoeuvrable. The small cockpit gave the instructor in the rear seat a limited forward view. However, it offered the advanced student all the high-speed performance training – being transonic in a shallow dive – whilst providing the low-speed and landing characteristics required for training and operations in all weather conditions. Gnats remained as the RAF's standard advanced trainer until superseded by the Hawk at Valley in November 1978.

Squadron Leader Ray Hanna, member of the original team and former leader of the *Red Arrows* recalls his early days on the jet trainer, 'The Gnat was the second, maybe third generation jet, with powered controls, swept wings and with all sorts of modern avionics very similar to the Lightning. My first impressions of the Gnat were just that it was totally delightful, and very, very sensitive after the Meteor. In a sense it was much nicer to fly than, say, the Hunter, and of course the two aircraft were always being directly compared. It suffered from lack of

Above: From 1965 to 1979 Gnat T2s equipped the RAF's premier aerobatic display team, the *Red Arrows*. The aircraft were painted in a distinctive all-red colour scheme.

thrust over 25,000ft but low down it had all that was necessary. The low wing loading made it a very manoeuvrable aeroplane, particularly at low altitude, but it did bump around in turbulence. It was a totally delightful aeroplane, and during the five years at the *Red Arrows*, it never suffered any major failure or major accident.'

Right: Forerunner of the *Red Arrows*, the *Yellowjacks Gnat* display team formed at RAF Valley in 1964. Its aircraft were painted yellow overall, like this aircraft that is still flying in 1998.

POWERPLANT: One 18.83kN (4230lb st) Bristol Siddeley Orpheus 100 turbojet
SPAN: 7.32m (24ft 0in); Length: 9.68m (31ft 9in)
MAX SPEED: 1024km/h (636mph)
ACCOMMODATION: Two seats in tandem
FIRST AIRCRAFT FLOWN: 18 July 1955 (single-seat prototype); 31 August 1959 (T1)
ENTERED RAF SERVICE: February 1962 (T1, Central Flying School)
LAST RAF SERVICE: September 1979 (T1, Red Arrows).

1962

WESTLAND WESSEX

When the RAF required a replacement for its Whirlwinds, it followed the Royal Navy's lead and ordered the Westland Wessex, a turbine-engined version of the Sikorsky S-58. Designated as the Wessex HC2 in RAF service, with its twin-coupled Gnome turbines it has been used for troop-carrying, casualty evacuation, search and rescue, communications and general purposes duties. It can cruise with one engine inoperative, and lift up to sixteen fully-equipped troops or a 1818kg (4000lb) underslung load.

The design of the twin-engine hatch bay made both units easily accessible, and either engine can be removed without reference to the other. The naval features of folding rotors and tails on the Wessex in RAF service enabled maximum use to be made of small clearings in woodland in which to hide the tactical support helicopters.

The Wessex HC2 arrived in squadron service with No 18 at Odiham in 1964. Today, just two squadrons remain operational with the helicopter. No 72 Squadron that has been at RAF Aldergrove, Northern Ireland since 1981 and No 84 Squadron at Akrotiri in Cyprus, operating there since 1982.

The Wessex HC2 initially equipped search and rescue flights of No 22 Squadron in 1976, these yellow-painted machines becoming familiar and

Left: Flying along the water-front at Hong Kong, a Wessex HC2 of No 28 Squadron that served until the British handover in June 1997.

Below: Two specially equipped Wessex HCC4s were operated as VIP transports with the Queen's Flight from June 1969 until retired from No 32 (The Royal) Squadron at RAF Northolt in 1998.

Above: Yellow-painted Wessex HC2s were used for search and rescue duties with Nos 22 and 202 Squadrons, the former operating the helicopter from mid-1976 until the last one was replaced by a Sea King in 1997.

welcome sights around the coastline as the Whirlwinds had been before them. However, the last SAR Wessex was retired in favour of Sea Kings, in 1997.

Two Wessex were specially furnished and equipped internally for service with the Queen's Flight. Designated HCC4, they were painted bright red and served for nearly 30 years with the Queen's Flight and No 32 (The Royal) Squadron at RAF Northolt.

The Captain of the Queen's Flight recalls Wessex operations, 'The workload is shared equally between the three crews who man the two Wessex HCC4s. However, HRH The Duke of Edinburgh and HRH The Prince of Wales have personal pilots allocated to them, who invariably fly with them. The Duke of Edinburgh always pilots the helicopter himself, and quite frequently so does The Prince of Wales. Royal helicopter flights rarely start and finish at airfields. On

the contrary, our pick up points are usually in Central London or at one of the Royal residences scattered across the country and our destination could be anywhere, literally anywhere!'

POWERPLANT: Two coupled 1006kW (1350shp) Bristol Siddeley Gnome (one Mk 110 and one Mk 111) shaft turbines
ROTOR DIAMETER: 17.06m (56ft 0in); Fuselage length: 20.04m (65ft 9in)
Max speed: 213km/h (132mph)
ACCOMMODATION: Crew of two/three; capacity for 16 troops in cabin. Ground assault version carried Nord anti-tank missiles and machine guns
FIRST AIRCRAFT FLOWN: 17 May 1957 (RN HAS1)
ENTERED RAF SERVICE: January 1964 (HC2, No 18 Squadron); still current.

BAC VC10

Above: Tanker trail – VC10 K2 of No 101 Squadron refuelling a pair of Harrier GR7s from RAF Wittering.

Right: Sunset on the tow-line. A VC10 K3 of No 101 Squadron awaits thirsty Tornado F3s during an exercise off northern Scotland.

With the arrival of the VC10 C1 in 1966, the RAF obtained a significant addition to the strategic long-range fleet of Transport Command and its airlift capacity. At the time it was the heaviest aircraft to enter the RAF inventory and offered global mobility with a speed, capacity and higher productive capacity factor better than any other transport aircraft. Rear-facing seats were fitted, as was a side-loading freight door and refuelling probe. Fourteen C1s were delivered to No 10 Squadron at RAF Brize Norton, all named after airman recipients of the Victoria Cross.

At their peak service they operated twenty-seven flights each month to the Far East, via the Persian Gulf. Defence economies from 1975 resulted in No 10 Squadron slowly relinquishing its regular, world-

Left: Dawn patrol. A VC10 K3 refuelling a pair of Tornado F3s high over the North Sea while on combat air patrol.

POWERPLANT: Four 96.97kN (21,800lb st) Rolls-Royce Conway 301 turbofans (C1K)
SPAN: 44.55m (146ft 2in); **Length:** 48.38m (158ft 8in)
MAX SPEED: 935km/h (581mph)
ACCOMMODATION: Crew of four; can carry 150 passengers or seventy-six stretchers
FIRST AIRCRAFT FLOWN: 29 June 1962
ENTERED RAF SERVICE: July 1966 (C1, No 10 Squadron); still current.

Above: Inside the cockpit of a VC10 tanker.

Overleaf: Pilot's eye view from a VC10 tanker.

wide transport schedule. From the mid-1990s the C1s gained a new lease of life when they were converted to C1K standard, with a dual role as tanker/transports.

With the growing importance of in-flight refuelling, and the impending retirement of the Victor K2, the VC10 was chosen as the principal equipment of the future tanker fleet, and ex-civil aircraft were purchased. British Aerospace at Filton carried out the conversions – the first delivery being made in 1984. These were followed ten years later by five further Super VC10 conversions. Primarily intended to refuel air defence fighters, such as Phantoms and Tornados, the VC10s incorporated two underwing hose drum units, and a third in the rear fuselage. Flying with No 101 Squadron they were heavily utilized during the Gulf War, and subsequently over Bosnia, and in the Gulf region. The RAF's VC10 tanker force comprises twenty-six aircraft – twelve C1Ks and five K2s, four K3s and five K4s all based at Brize Norton.

Flight Lieutenant Nick Wilcock, a VC10K pilot who flew thirty-eight operational tanking sorties during Operation *Desert Storm* in 1991, recorded, 'Peacetime training had been totally vindicated in war. The invaluable worldwide experience gained in Red Flag and Far East deployments had enabled crews to adapt rapidly to the changing requirements of the war. The VC10 had proved to be highly reliable. A total of 600 sorties were flown prior to 16 January, off-loading 14,000 tonnes fuel; after 16 January 381 sorties (1350hr) were flown with a further 6800 tonnes given away. The reliability of Flight Refuelling Ltd's AAR equipment proved to be outstanding in a very demanding environment, no VC10K mission having failed due to refuelling equipment malfunction. With over 90% of all RAF attack and air defence missions needing AAR, without the tanker force it would have been totally impossible for the RAF to have enjoyed the success in the Gulf which it did.'

HAWKER SIDDELEY ANDOVER

Above: After being retired as transports several Andovers were fitted with radio and radar calibrating equipment, painted in this bright colour scheme and operated as Andover E3s by No 115 Squadron until October 1993.

The RAF had an operational requirement for a Valetta and Hastings replacement with short take-off and landing (STOL) capability, available for troop transport, paratroop dropping, aerial delivery of supplies, freighting and aero-medical evacuation. In competition with the Handley Page Herald, Hawker Siddeley was awarded the contract for the HS748 Andover C1 in 1964.

The transport was able to operate from rough air strips or desert runways. The C1, of which thirty-one were supplied, featured a lengthened fuselage with rear loading facilities and a 'beaver tail' for air dropping. A 'kneeling undercarriage' enabled the fuselage angle to be lowered so that vehicles could be driven off and on over the rear-loading ramp. It served overseas in the Far East and at Aden and

Bahrain until 1971. A small number continued with No 60 Squadron in Germany until March 1992.

Six Andover CC2s were built for the RAF, furnished purely for passenger carrying and retaining the civil HS748 configuration. Two entered service with the Queen's Flight and the others went initially to RAF communications flights overseas. The CC2s were retired from No 32 (The Royal) Squadron in March 1995.

A Queen's Flight engineer talked about the Andover CC2 in the 1980s, "We had to provide three one hundred per cent serviceable Andovers in immaculate condition to meet about 800 Royal Flights a year. We ensured that whenever they flew, they could not only be operated with maximum safety but also depart and arrive within five seconds of

Below: A replacement for the Valetta transport, the Andover C1 was in service with No 46 Squadron at Abingdon from September 1966. It could operate from unprepared airstrips with a short take-off and landing performance.

their planned time. The Flight's technicians were amongst the finest in the RAF and the standards laid down, and consistently met, were among the most exacting. We were considerably assisted in our task by the proven reliability and ease of maintenance of both the Dart engine and the Andover airframe. The aircraft often spent weeks away, operating from small, remote airfields in far-flung continents. The Andovers were constantly in the public eye and needed to be fit for a Queen inside and out, so they were always kept in immaculate condition.'

A handful of Andover C1s were equipped with special electronic equipment and used by No 115 Squadron from November 1976 as the E3. They replaced the Argosy E1 on calibration duties. On disbandment of No 115 Squadron in October 1993, the E3s were transferred to Hunting Aviation Services at East Midlands Airport.

POWERPLANT: Two 2476kW (3245shp) Rolls-Royce Dart RDa12 Mk 201C turboprops (Andover C1)
SPAN: 27.43m (90ft 0in); Length: 23.74m (77ft 11in)
MAX SPEED: 487km/h (302mph)
ACCOMMODATION: Crew of three; room for forty-four troops, thirty fully equipped paratroops, eighteen stretchers or 6364kg (14,000lb) of freight (C1)
FIRST AIRCRAFT FLOWN: 9 July 1961 (Avro 748); 9 July 1965 (Andover C1)
ENTERED RAF SERVICE: December 1966 (C1, No 46 Squadron)
LAST RAF SERVICE: 1996 (E3, Hunting Aviation Services).

LOCKHEED HERCULES

Above: In the early 1980s, twenty-nine C-130Ks had their fuselages lengthened. This Hercules C3 can accommodate up to thirty-six more troops than the ninety-two carried by the original C1.

Right: RAF Hercules from Lyneham have been called upon to assist aid agencies with humanitarian relief in many parts of the world since the C-130K entered service in 1967.

In August 1954 a new four-engined transport aircraft made its maiden flight at Burbank, California and in the four decades since, the Lockheed C-130 Hercules has become a legend. It has operated in all parts of the globe in all conditions, undertaking a greater variety of missions than any other type of aircraft, and its production run for countless air arms looks set to continue well into the 21st century. In replacing the Hastings and Beverley, the RAF's C-130K fleet, which started operations in 1967, gave the service a tactical airlift capability which has proved invaluable in war and peace.

Changes have occurred to the Hercules in RAF service to provide greater operating capacity. The most significant of these resulted in the Hercules C3,

Right: A single RAF Hercules
W2 (XV208) was specially
modified for weather research and
reconnaissance and flown from
Farnborough and Boscombe
Down. Because of its extended
nose probe it was dubbed
Snoopy.

with its fuselage stretched by fifteen feet. Nearly half
the original fleet of sixty-six aircraft were brought to
this configuration by Marshall of Cambridge, the last
being re-delivered in 1985. They also undertook the
modification of six aircraft to C1K tanker standard.
The whole of the Lyneham based fleet was given in-
flight refuelling probes. One aircraft was modified for
weather research and air sampling. With its extended
nose and cabin top radar it was appropriately named
Snoopy. Set to enter RAF service in 1999, the C-130J
Hercules, has a new 'glass' cockpit, head-up displays,
much improved avionics and Allison AE2100
turboprops driving scythe-shaped, six-blade
propellers. The RAF is purchasing fifteen stretched
C4s and ten standard length C5s.

Wing Commander Tony Webb, who took part
in Operation *Agila* recounted some of his experiences
of flying the Hercules in the former Rhodesia. 'The
operation lasted for over three months and Operation
Agila provided an outstanding example of the

adaptability of the Hercules. The confidence in the
aircraft and the remarkable resilience it gave to crews
is a tribute to Lockheed's excellent aeroplane. Other
aspects of reliability were underlined by the
astonishingly high success of the daily programme.'

POWERPLANT: Four 3362kW (4508eshp) Allison T56-
A-15 turboprops
SPAN: 40.41m (132ft 7in); Length: 29.79m (97ft 9in)
MAX SPEED: 602km/h (374mph)
ACCOMMODATION: Crew of four or six and up to 92
troops, 64 paratroops or 74 stretchers; maximum
payload of 19,397kg (42,675lb)
FIRST AIRCRAFT FLOWN:
 23 August 1954 (YC-130); 19 October 1966 (RAF C-
130K Hercules C1)
ENTERED RAF SERVICE: December 1966 (C1, No 242
OCU); still current.

McDONNELL DOUGLAS PHANTOM

When Britain threw its own combat aircraft projects, including the supersonic Hawker P1154, on the scrap-heap in 1964 and 1965 and bought the Phantom, the decision was taken to install the Rolls-Royce Spey turbofan. This engine had to be restressed for supersonic flight, given an afterburner and variable nozzle and developed in other ways from the version fitted to the Buccaneer. One pilot wrote, 'When you watch the Phantom take off, you see her arched nose and down-swept stabilator separated by a bulky midriff that looks as awkward as a goose with drooping tail feathers and a middle-aged spread.' Another was even more outspoken, 'When I first saw a Phantom I thought it so ugly I wondered if it had been delivered upside-down.' They all changed their views after it entered service.

The RAF had two versions, the FG1 air defence interceptor (transferred from the Royal Navy) and the FGR2, that flew in the ground attack and tactical reconnaissance role. In the 1970s and 1980s, almost daily Phantoms had to scramble to intercept long-range Soviet Tu-95 'Bear' electronic reconnaissance

1968

Above: Armed to the teeth, a
Phantom FGR2 on combat air
patrol over Germany at the height
of the Cold War.

Previous page: This highly
decorated Phantom FGR2 was
flown across the Atlantic by
Squadron Leader A J Alcock and
Flight Lieutenant W S Browne in
1979 to mark the 60th anniversary
of the first crossing by their name
sakes, Messrs. Alcock and Brown
in a Vickers Vimy.

Right: A Phantom of No 56
Squadron, the penultimate unit to
fly the fighter for UK air defence,
shortly before it was disbanded in
July 1992.

platforms carrying on the ceaseless game of listening
and probing.

When the Jaguar began to serve in the ground
attack role, the Phantom FGR2s were passed to Strike
Command's fighter squadrons. With the demands on
the interceptor fighter after the Falklands conflict,
there was a shortage of F-4s with the home-based
units. No 74 Squadron was reformed at Wattisham in
1984 and fifteen secondhand US Navy F-4Js were
purchased, becoming known as F-4J(UK)s and
retaining their General Electric J79 turbojets. These
aircraft remained on strength until 1991. Following
the service entry of the Tornado F3 from 1987, the
Phantom was progressively phased out. RAF
Germany's last Phantoms, those of Nos 19 and 92
Squadrons at Wildenrath, were finally stood down in

POWERPLANT: Two 54.55kN (12,250lb st); 91.41kN
(20,525lb st) Rolls-Royce RB 16825R Spey 202 by-
pass turbofans with reheat
SPAN: 11.70m (38ft 4.75in); Length: 17.55m (57ft
7in)
MAX SPEED: 2235km/h (1386mph)
Typical armament: Interception – Four Sky Flash or
Sparrow medium-range AAMs and four Sidewinder
short-range AAMs; Ground attack – Eleven 454kg
(1000lb) free-fall or retarded bombs, 126 SNEB
68mm armour-piercing rockets. One 20mm Vulcan
SUU23 rotary cannon on all aircraft
FIRST AIRCRAFT FLOWN: 27 May 1958 (USN F4H-
1); 17 February 1967 (RAF F-4M)
ENTERED RAF SERVICE: 23 August 1968 (FGR2, No
228 OCU)
LAST RAF SERVICE: October 1992 (FGR2, No 74
Squadron).

January 1992, and the last squadron in the UK, No 74
at Wattisham, retired its Phantom FGR2s the
following October.

HAWKER SIDDELEY/
BAe HARRIER

There can be no doubt that the Harrier family and the Rolls-Royce Pegasus series of vectored-thrust turbofans, together formed Britain's most important contribution to post-war military aviation technology. Until some time well into the next century the British Aerospace/ McDonnell Douglas Harrier family will continue to represent the world's only high performance V/STOL combat aircraft to see service on a significant scale, just as its Pegasus powerplant will remain the only series-built engine of its type.

The decision to equip the RAF with Harriers, that it did not want, was a controversial one and it was to take several years for the service to accept fully that it really did provide unique survivability when operating from dispersed sites in Germany. In RAF service, the primary role of the Harrier was to attack second-echelon armoured units in the face of relatively advanced air defences. Operating at high subsonic speed, and mainly at low-level, its BL755 cluster weapons and 68mm SNEB rockets required more height in the attack phase.

Hawker Chief Test Pilot, A W 'Bill' Bedford famously described the capability of the prototype vertical take-off and landing aircraft with his first deck landing on a ship in the P.1127. 'In 1963 the British

Right: Developed jointly by British Aerospace and McDonnell Douglas, the Harrier II featured a new carbonfibre composite wing, better performance and armament than its predecessor. This Harrier GR7, introduced in 1990 currently serves with three RAF front-line squadrons and the OCU.

1969

1969

Right: The Harrier demonstrates its unique survivability when operating from dispersed sites.

Left: Wearing a grey paint scheme for operations over northern Iraq this Harrier GR7 is based at Wittering.

Government had decided in the longer-term to deny the Royal Navy the use of aircraft carriers. It was in this climate that we obtained somewhat reluctant authorization to try out the P.1127 on HMS *Ark Royal*. On 8 February 1963 snow and ice had grounded all conventional aircraft in our area. Whilst we were confident that the exercise would be successful, there were certain prophets of doom from the Ministry who made comments, such as, "Beware the cliff edge effect and the hot air from the funnel, mind the turbulence from behind the island; what happens if the nozzles do not come down or if the engine stops; you might buckle the deck or blow the crew overboard, or even deafen them!" In the event it was a complete anti-climax and emphasized the comparative ease of operating V/STOL aircraft from ships. I landed aboard effortlessly and vertically, thus making the first ever fixed-wing jet V/STOL operations from a ship.'

The initial GR1 became the GR3 in 1976, when it acquired a Laser Ranger and Marked-Target Seeker nose and the uprated Pegasus 11 engine. The two-seat T2 conversion trainer variant thus became the T4. One UK-based front-line squadron and the Operational Conversion Unit, all at RAF Wittering, were augmented by three (later two) units in Germany, and the type's first combat action came in the Falklands in 1982. During the conflict, fourteen Harrier GR3s accompanied twenty-eight Royal Navy Sea Harriers to the South Atlantic and were

Above: The GR7's nose profile includes Forward-Looking Infra-Red on top, with the Hughes AN/ASB–19(V) Angle Rate Bombing set below.

Right: Harrier GR7's operated from Gioia del Colle, Italy, from August 1995 as part of Operation *Deny Flight*.

POWERPLANT: One 96.86kN (21,750lb st) Rolls-Royce Pegasus 105 vectored-thrust turbofan (GR7)
SPAN: 9.24m (30ft 4in); Length: 14.36m (47ft 1_in)
MAX SPEED: 1066km/h (661mph)
TYPICAL ARMAMENT: Twin 25mm Aden guns, two AIM-9L Sidewinder AAMs, plus 4,181kg (9,200lb) of weapons on seven pylons
FIRST AIRCRAFT FLOWN: 21 October 1960 (P1127); 31 August 1966 (GR1)
ENTERED RAF SERVICE: July 1969 (GR1, No 1 Squadron); GR7 and T10 still current.

used in the ground attack role, flying over 150 missions.

The GR5, the first of the second-generation Harrier IIs, entered RAF service in May 1987. This was modified to the definitive GR7, which was specifically tailored to operate equally effectively at night as it could during reasonable daytime weather. Re-equipment in Germany was accompanied by a change of tasking priority. As a senior pilot stated on service entry of the GR7, 'We have to get away from the Harrier being seen as an aircraft which flies twenty-minute sorties out of a wood.'

HAWKER SIDDELEY BUCCANEER

T he notorious Defence White Paper of April 1957 proclaimed manned combat aircraft obsolete, but the Blackburn B103, built to meet the naval attack specification NA39, was the only new British military aircraft not cancelled. Designed for carrier operations it featured boundary–layer control, achieved by blasting hot compressed air bled from the engines from narrow slits.

The first eighty-four were ordered by the Royal

Above: The last RAF Buccaneers were retired in March 1994.

Right: Equipped with Sea Eagle anti-ship weapons, these two Buccaneers are from Nos 12 and 208 Squadrons, the last two units to fly the low-level strike aircraft.

1969

Left: The Buccaneer was one of the RAF's most cost-effective aircraft.

Above: A Buccaneer S2B of No 12 Squadron flying from its base at RAF Lossiemouth, Scotland.

Navy and most of these were subsequently transferred to RAF Strike Command after October 1969. Following the ill-advised cancellation of the TSR2, forty-three new Buccaneer S2Bs were delivered to the RAF. Though not initially over-enthusiastic about the Buccaneer, the RAF found the aircraft strong and unbreakable and proved one of the most cost effective aircraft ever designed for tactical use.

The Buccaneer served in Germany, replacing Canberras, and were deployed in a low-level penetration role in support of NATO's Supreme

POWERPLANT: Two 49.87kN (11,200lb st) Rolls-Royce RB168 Spey M turbofans (S2B)
SPAN: 13.41m (44ft 0in); Length: 19.33m (63ft 5in)
MAX SPEED: 1038km/h (645mph)
TYPICAL ARMAMENT: Total warload 7272kg (16,000lb) carried on wing pylons and in the fuselage bomb bay, comprising combinations of 454kg (1000lb) iron bombs or laser-guided bombs. Maritime strike role; Sea Eagle or Martel anti-ship weapons
FIRST AIRCRAFT FLOWN: 30 April 1958 (RN NA39)
ENTERED RAF SERVICE: October 1969 (S2, No 12 Squadron)
LAST RAF SERVICE: April 1994 (S2B, No 208 Squadron).

Allied Commander Europe, pending the arrival of the Tornado GR1. From the early 1980s, Strike Command's Buccaneers continued to fly on maritime strike and reconnaissance duties, and in 1983 executed sorties from Cyprus during the Lebanon crisis.

Operation *Desert Storm* enabled the old, but still potent, Buccaneer to enjoy an 'Indian Summer' when it played a vital role using its Pave Spike laser designator equipment to support Tornado GR1 strikes, especially in the destruction of bridges over the River Euphrates in Iraq. They directed 169 LGBs to destroy twenty-four key bridges and successfully attacked fourteen airfields where hardened aircraft shelters were demolished and runways effectively destroyed.

An RAF Buccaneer pilot from the 'Desert Pirates' said: 'Of all the RAF elements in *Desert Storm*, the Buccaneer force proved the most vital and the fastest to respond. Without the help of a thirty-year old bomber – more at home skimming the cold

waters between the UK and Iceland than at medium altitude over Iraq's arid wastes – Tornados would have spent the war scattering 454kg (1000lb) bombs only slightly more accurately than did Lancasters in World War II. Buccaneers allowed the Tornado force to regain the accuracy of attack lost when missions were transferred to above 20,000ft to evade SAMs and AAA surrounding targets. Like many aircraft in the war, the aged Buccaneer was fighting its last campaign.'

Back in the UK the Lossiemouth Maritime Strike Wing was due for imminent change and No 12 Squadron retired its Buccaneers in October 1993, receiving Tornado GR1Bs in exchange. No 208 Squadron relinquished its Buccaneers in April 1994. They were replaced by the Tornados of No 617 Squadron, thus ending the twenty-five year career of the RAF's last all-British bomber aircraft in front-line service.

HAWKER SIDDELEY NIMROD

Below: Flying near to the 'Old Man of Hoy', this Nimrod MR2 is carrying a chaff dispenser (BOZ pod) under its starboard wing and a Sidewinder air-to-air missile.

Developed from the de Havilland Comet, the Nimrod maritime patrol aircraft was designed to replace the Avro Shackleton. A weapons pannier was added beneath the cabin, giving a distinctive 'double-bubble' cross section, which necessitated an increase in fin area. A magnetic anomaly detector (MAD) 'stinger' was added to the tailcone, a search radar to the nose and a fin-top radar to house ESM equipment.

Originally the Nimrod MR1 equipped five squadrons in the UK (the first being delivered in October 1969) and one based in the Mediterranean. The British withdrawal from Malta rendered these eight aircraft surplus, and some were used for the

abortive AEW3 programme. In the mid–1970s the initial MR1 versions began to be upgraded to MR2 standard with much enhanced electronics and the addition of in-flight refuelling probes. The Falklands War resulted in underwing hardpoints being used by front-line Nimrods for the first time, carrying AIM-9 Sidewinders. Wingtip Loral ESM pods were also added.

Nimrods played an important part in the Falklands conflict and the Gulf War. Flight Lieutenant Tony Cowan described a long-range sortie from Ascension Island during the Falklands Conflict. 'On 15 May 1982, we took off in Nimrod MR2 XV232 and 201 Squadron crew 7 at 0857 for a flight which

1969

lasted 19hr 5min, extensive cloud having prevented the use of satellite-derived information. We flew south to a point 150 miles north of Port Stanley and then west until approximately 60 miles off the Argentine coast. XV232 then tracked north-east at between 7000ft and 12,000ft parallel with the coast and its Searchwater radar was used to survey a strip 400 miles wide and 1000 miles long, confirming that all Argentine warships were still successfully blockaded in port by the threat of British nuclear-powered submarines. It was a fine day and the aircraft was vulnerable during some segments of that flight, but the Nimrod was successfully recovered to Wideawake without incident after a total of three AARs and having travelled 8300 miles. This was the longest sortie by any aircraft during Operation *Corporate* and one of the longest RAF missions of all time.'

Left: Three squadrons of Nimrod MR2s are based at RAF Kinloss.

POWERPLANT: Four 53.41kN (11,995lb st) Rolls-Royce Spey 250 turbofans
SPAN: 35.00m (114ft 10in); Length: 38.63m (126ft 9in)
MAX SPEED: 926km/h (575mph)
TYPICAL ARMAMENT: Nine Mk44 or 46 homing torpedoes, or Marconi Stingray torpedoes, in bomb bay; alternatively nuclear depth charges or conventional 454kg (1000lb) iron bombs; provision to carry two Harpoon air-to-surface missiles, and up to four AIM-9 Sidewinders for self-defence.
AIRCRAFT FIRST FLOWN: 23 May 1967
ENTERED RAF SERVICE: 1 October 1969 (MR1, No 236 OTU); MR2 and R1 still current.

Below: One of the longest-serving front-line RAF types, the Hawker Siddeley Nimrod long-range maritime reconnaissance aircraft has been on operational strength since July 1970.

WESTLAND PUMA

A product of a joint Anglo–French manufacturing agreement, the Puma was developed from the Aerospatiale SA300. Forty-eight Pumas were built for the RAF by Westland at Hayes in the early 1970s. It was designed for a wide range of duties, including casualty evacuation, troop transport and as a helicopter gunship. The type's twin doors and spacious cabin make the type popular with its Army users, who also appreciate its versatility.

The Puma has proved invaluable in the Army support role, especially as it can carry underslung loads, such as light field guns. A squadron was set up for Operation *Desert Storm* in 1991, and nineteen Pumas were deployed to the Gulf, camouflaged in desert pink livery. They have also seen active service in Belize and been used on mercy missions in Bosnia and Zambia. Since 1992, Pumas have been used in support of the British Army's operations in Northern Ireland. It has also served with the Army in Germany, Cyprus, Zimbabwe and on NATO exercises in Norway.

An RAF Puma pilot reported on the Puma deployment to the Gulf: 'A composite RAF Puma

Below: Equipped with front and rear radar warning receivers, this Puma of No 33 Squadron shows the latest operational configuration for the tactical assault and troop transport helicopter.

Right: Pumas from Nos 33 and 230 Squadrons took part in the Gulf War providing support to British Army Units during the campaign in 1991.

1971

POWERPLANT: Two 984kW (1320shp) Turboméca Turmo 111C4 shaft-turbines
ROTOR DIAMETER: 14.99m (49ft 2.5in); Fuselage length: 14.75m (48ft 5in)
Max speed: 280km/h (174mph)
ACCOMMODATION: Crew of two and up to sixteen troops
FIRST AIRCRAFT FLOWN: 15 April 1965 (SA330)
ENTERED RAF SERVICE: June 1971 (HC1, No 33 Squadron); still current.

squadron was assembled from No 33 Squadron at Odiham and No 230 Squadron from Gütersloh, Germany. We air-freighted the majority from RAF Brize Norton in USAF Lockheed C-5s and initially operated from Ras al Ghar. Our prime duty involved carriage of up to sixteen troops or 2.5 tonnes of underslung loads, such as ammunition. We remained close to the troops, leaving Jubail for King Khalid Military City (KKMC) on 20 January and then proceeded westward as General Schwarzkopf's "left-hook" thrust into Iraq was prepared. Night-vision goggles were regularly used and the uprated navigation equipment proved a godsend in the featureless terrain. The coalition advance in the land war beginning 24 February was so swift that ground-refuelling and re-arming parties had difficulty in keeping up with the helicopters as they accompanied the leading elements of UK forces deep into Iraq.'

A recent upgrade has dramatically reduced the aircraft's vulnerability to hostile ground fire. Improvements include updated missile approach warning detection, IR detection and flare dispensers, as well as better avionics.

Left: Pumas on exercise with the British Army, a support role that they have fulfilled since June 1971 when they first equipped No 33 Squadron.

SEPECAT JAGUAR

The Jaguar was produced by the international company SEPECAT – a collaborative venture between the then British Aircraft Corporation and the French company Dassault-Breguet. It was designed to meet dual Anglo–French requirements for a supersonic strike/attack aircraft and advanced trainer, operating in the northern Europe theatre. The RAF acquired a total of 203 Jaguars fitted with a very accurate attack system to operate at low level. At its peak in the mid-seventies it equipped eight front-line RAF squadrons from 1974 replacing Phantoms as a major element in RAF Germany's tactical air capability, until the arrival of the Tornado in 1985.

Wing Command John Walker, Officer Commanding the Jaguar Operational Conversion Unit in the early 1970s, described the aircraft as, 'A very high performance little ship. It certainly gets out and gets up very fast indeed – to the point that it surprises Lightning pilots. For the first time we have got an aircraft where you can virtually guarantee, on interdiction-type targets, making the very fast, low-level, straight-pass attack. The aim of weapons delivery is to put the bomb on the target, and that's what Jaguar does better than anything else we have.'

The first RAF attack aircraft to be sent to the Gulf following Iraq's invasion of Kuwait, the Jaguar GR1A served throughout *Desert Storm* without an aircraft

Below: Jaguar GR1s taxi in to their dispersal at RAF Coltishall, home base for the RAF's single-seat tactical support, ground-attack and reconnaissance aircraft since 1974.

1973

Left: Desert camouflaged Jaguar GR1As from the Coltishall Wing made a major contribution to the Gulf War, flying over 600 daylight sorties on strike missions over Iraq.

Above: A Jaguar GR1A of No 54 Squadron carrying AIM-9P Sidewinder self-defence air-to-air missiles on overwing pylons, introduced during the Gulf War.

POWERPLANT: Two 32.73kN (7305lb st) Rolls-Royce/Turboméca RT172 Adour 104 turbofans (GR1A)
SPAN: 8.68m (28ft 6in); Length: 16.82m (55ft 2_in)
MAX SPEED: 1596km/h (990mph)
TYPICAL ARMAMENT: Two 30mm Aden guns; provision for up to 4773kg (10,500lb) on five hardpoints, including bombs and rockets, two over-wing AIM-9P Sidewinder SRAAMs for self-defence
FIRST AIRCRAFT FLOWN: September 1968
ENTERED RAF SERVICE: September 1973 (GR1, No 226 OCU); still current.

being lost through enemy action. The twelve Jaguars deployed were fitted with overwing rails for self-defence AIM-9L Sidewinders. Main 'trade' for the JagDet was forays to Republican Guard encampments, 'Silkworm' coastal-defence missile batteries, landing craft and targets in Iraq itself. Although the Jaguar had eighteen years of service behind them they still proved to be one of the most cost-effective weapons in the RAF's strike armoury.

At Incirlik, in Turkey, Jaguars operated until April 1993 as part of Operation *Warden* to defend the Kurds in Northern Iraq. The aircraft then continued their support of UN duties, within the NATO deployment to Italy at Gioia del Celle, supporting Operation *Grapple* over Bosnia. Some later participated, alongside Harrier GR7s, in Operation *Deliberate Force*.

Below and right: The Jaguar remains in front-line service twenty-five years after it was first introduced.

BAe HAWK

Right: Still in production as a two-seat advanced trainer for overseas air arms, the BAe Hawk has provided invaluable service to the RAF since first introduced in November 1976 at No 4FTS at RAF Valley. Its role as an operational and weapons trainer has been equally important.

In the late 1960s the RAF realized the need to replace the Gnat and Hunter, in both advanced flying and weapons training roles. The service was looking for an aircraft to train pilots in all aspects of fast-jet operations, by day and night, before proceeding to their operational squadrons equipped with the Tornado, Jaguar, Phantom and Harrier.

The Hawk was gradually delivered into RAF service beginning in 1976. Four units initially received the new trainer – RAF Valley for advanced flying training, RAF Brawdy and RAF Chivenor for tactical weapons training and the RAF aerobatic team, the *Red Arrows*. Eighty-eight Hawk T1s were subsequently modified to carry AIM-9 Sidewinder air-to-air missiles for second-line defence of UK installations, designated as Hawk T1As.

Today No 4 FTS at Valley has three Reserve Squadrons under its wing incorporating all elements of the advanced fast jet training and weapons instruction syllabus. The other current RAF Hawk unit is Leeming-based No 100 Squadron, the first to perform the 'aggressor' role in the RAF, while other examples have been assigned to the Institute of Aviation Medicine and Empire Test Pilots School at Boscombe Down.

Below: Hawks replaced Gnats with the *Red Arrows* aerobatic display team in 1979. They remain in service with the team nearly twenty years later.

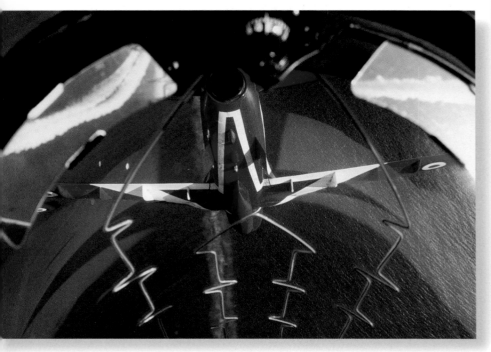

238

1976

The good handling characteristics of the Hawk have been convincingly, and expertly, demonstrated to the world by the *Red Arrows* aerobatic team. Equally important factors in the aircraft's success are the simplicity and durability of the Hawk's airframe, its operational reliability and its low cost maintenance. Added to this is true mission flexibility, low fuel consumption and a robust and uncomplicated design. The rear cockpit is raised to provide the flying instructor with an exceptional field of view, thus enabling him to monitor the actions of the student and see the touchdown point during landing.

Squadron Leader Andy Wyatt, a former *Red Arrows* and qualified flying instructor gives his view of the handling qualities of the Hawk, 'The Hawk was a big step-up from the Jet Provost – particularly in terms of speed – and the tandem cockpit layout really gives you the impression of being on your own in a single-seat aeroplane. It has a well laid-out cockpit, where everything falls nicely to hand. Visibility is excellent from both cockpits and the fuel economy of the Adour engine, particularly at altitude, is very good, but the aircraft's high speed, low-level ride, can be bumpy.'

Left: The all-black colour scheme was adopted for all RAF training Hawks in 1994.

Right: The *Red Arrows* final rehearsals for each season are conducted in Cyprus.

POWERPLANT: One 23.15kN (5200lb st) Rolls-Royce/Turboméca Adour Mk 151 turbofan
SPAN: 9.39m (39ft 10in); Length: 11.85m (38ft 10in)
MAX SPEED: 1068km/h (662mph)
TYPICAL ARMAMENT: Two AIM-9L Sidewinder AAMs on inboard wing pylons and one 30mm Aden gun on fuselage centreline (T1A)
FIRST AIRCRAFT FLOWN: 21 August 1974
ENTERED RAF SERVICE: 4 November 1976 (T1, No 4 FTS); still current.

WESTLAND SEA KING

The first Westland-built Sea King made its maiden flight in September 1967 and the early production examples went to the Royal Navy. In 1975, the RAF ordered sixteen HAR3 versions for the reorganisation of its SAR service, subsequently extended to twenty-two. When received the Sea King was the best-equipped rescue helicopter in service in terms of its avionics, that included the Decca TANS system in the cockpit, which was to prove of enormous value in difficult rescue operations.

The Sea King's normal capability is 250nm 'out-and-back' range with twelve survivors aboard. Initially doubts were expressed about Sea Kings being used for mountain rescue, as many experts considered them too big. Flight Lieutenant Bob King, an RAF Qualified Helicopter Instructor carried out exhaustive trials in the Cairngorms, Grampians and Isle of Skye. His report concluded: 'The Sea King is a good helicopter for mountain operations and provides a stable working platform. It should cope with most weathers and with careful handling and consideration can offer a high degree of safety. The downwash problem in the hills has shown itself not to be excessive and can be further reduced with careful handling. However, it would be wrong to completely minimize or even forget that a problem can exist.'

The primary role of the Sea King is to rescue downed aircrew from the sea or remote areas but they remain available as required to render assistance to civilian authorities in emergencies. Many dramatic rescues have been achieved, in all weather conditions including ice and snow, and at night using Nitesun equipment. Very-long-range sorties have included flights to Stavanger in Norway and to the Bay of Biscay. Since the Falklands conflict, Sea Kings have been based at Mount Pleasant with No 78 Squadron. In 1997, with the delivery of the new, up-dated Sea King 3A, the last of the RAF's yellow-painted SAR Wessex were replaced with No 22 Squadron's Flights at Chivenor and Wattisham.

Left: The new, improved Sea King HAR3A with a 'glass cockpit' and digital flight control system replaced the last Wessex HAR2s with No 22 Squadron in 1997.

Right: A newly delivered Sea King HAR3A of 'A' Flight, No 22 Squadron based at RMB Chivenor, engaged in the rescue of two teenage boys from rocks off Morenstow, Devon on 21 May 1997.

POWERPLANT: Two 1237kW (1660shp) Rolls-Royce Gnome H1400-1 shaft-turbines
ROTOR DIAMETER: 18.89m (62ft 0in); Fuselage length: 22.14m (72ft 8in)
MAX SPEED: 230km/h (143mph)
ACCOMMODATION: Crew of four and provision to carry nineteen passengers
FIRST AIRCRAFT FLOWN: 6 September 1977 (HAR3)
ENTERED RAF SERVICE: February 1978 (HAR3, Sea King Training Unit); still current.

BOEING VERTOL CHINOOK

The RAF's Support Helicopter Force is a key element of defence strategy in the post-Cold War era, providing air mobility and support for ground forces. RAF Odiham is the home base for most of the newly upgraded Chinook HC2 fleet and in the RAF's eightieth year is taking delivery of a further batch of new-build aircraft.

The tandem-rotor Chinook is fitted with a versatile triple hook system, which gives great flexibility with underslung loads. It can carry a streamlined rescue winch above the forward door and

Below: Chinook twin-rotor, medium-lift transport helicopters have provided invaluable battlefield support for the British Army since first introduced into service with No 18 Squadron at RAF Odiham in August 1981.

Below: In 1991 fifteen RAF Chinooks and their crews from Nos 7, 18 and 27 Squadrons played a major part in providing Army support during Operation *Desert Storm* in the Gulf.

a Nitesun searchlight in an articulated mounting below the nose. An auto-flight control and stability augmentation system is standard.

With its huge payload, almost three times greater than that of the Westland Puma, the Chinook makes a much-needed contribution to the RAF's heavy-lift capability in the battlefield support role. Prior to the ending of the Cold War, the Chinooks provided the British Army of the Rhine with its main airborne heavy-lift capability. It has also served with distinction in the Falklands, Lebanon and Operation *Desert Storm*. More recently they have been based in Turkey and operating for the United Nations in Bosnia.

Squadron Leader Ian Rose, a Flight Commander with the Rotary Wing Operational Evaluation and Training Unit comments on the Chinook. 'It takes more than learning to fly a Chinook for RAF Support Helicopter (SH) crews, who have to be capable of operating effectively, and to survive, in today's multi-threat battlefield environment. New global strategic concepts and rapid deployment force structures, all now rely on helicopters to provide much of their mobility and tactical flexibility. Chinooks have to undertake a wide range of missions from peace-keeping to a full regional conflict. It can carry M60D and M134 Miniguns, for gunnery sorties, the latter being purchased for the Gulf War. These had been manufactured and used by the US Army as a dedicated air-to-ground weapon. The Chinooks are now fully equipped with a comprehensive defensive aids suite, weapons and electronic countermeasures.'

POWERPLANT: Two 2237kW (3000shp) Textron Lycoming T-55-L-712 turboshafts
ROTOR DIAMETER: 18.29m (60ft 0in); Fuselage length: 15.54m (51ft 0in)
MAX SPEED: 290km/h (180mph)
ACCOMMODATION: Crew of four and thirty seated troops
FIRST AIRCRAFT FLOWN: 21 September 1961 (YCH-47)
ENTERED RAF SERVICE: December 1980 (HC1, No 240 OCU); still current.

PANAVIA TORNADO

Originally named the Multi-Role Combat Aircraft (MRCA), the Tornado emerged from a late 1960s tri-national feasibility study involving the BAC/BAe in the UK, Germany's MBB and Aeritalia in Italy. Panavia was formed in 1969 to build the aircraft, with formal development commencing in mid-1970. The variable-geometry MRCA prototype first flew in 1974, leading to the production Tornado IDS (Interdictor Strike) 'bomber', designated GR1 for RAF service. Power for the Tornado came from two Turbo-Union RB199 engines, developed by a consortium of Rolls-Royce, MTU and Fiat Avio.

Once in service with RAF Strike Command and RAF Germany in the early 1980s, the Tornado GR1 proved capable of delivering its warload with pinpoint accuracy in all weathers, day and night, using terrain-following radar to operate at low-level. The Air Defence Variant (ADV) came into full service in 1986 with the Sidewinder and Skyflash equipped Tornado F3.

Tornado GR1s and reconnaissance GR1As, made a major contribution to the Gulf War. They completed over 1500 bombing sorties, using ALARM anti-radar missiles, laser-guided bombs and JP233 low-level anti-runway weapons, helping to devastate Iraq's infrastructure.

Squadron Leader Dick Garwood, piloting GR1A ZA400 describes the first hunt sortie for Iraqi 'Scud' surface-to-air missiles on 18 January 1991. 'Our first mission was against the elusive mobile launchers from which the Scuds were being launched against Saudi

Below: Normally carrying four under-fuselage Skyflash MRAAMs, this Tornado F3 is firing one of four wing pylon-mounted AIM-9 Sidewinder SRAAMs that can also be carried for close-in targets.

1980

Arabia and threatening to bring Israel into the conflict. It was a very, very black night; probably one of the darkest I have flown on. Once you get out over the desert, especially over Iraq, there are no lights on the ground. We saw the odd Bedouin encampment flash by on the left-hand side of the wing. Flying at 200ft

Left: Introduced hurriedly into service during the Gulf War, ALARM (anti-radar) missiles were carried by sand-painted Tornado GR1s of No 9 Squadron. They are still available to RAF Tornados based in Kuwait.

Below: The first European consortium-designed strike aircraft, and the first with swing wings, replaced Buccaneers, Jaguars and the last Vulcans for overland bombing.

Left: A Tornado GR1B of No 12 Squadron, based at RAF Lossiemouth, equipped with Sea Eagle missiles for anti-shipping strike missions.

with "hard" ride selected on the terrain–following radar, and at speeds between 540 and 580kt, the sortie lasted two hours, involving nearly sixty minutes over Iraq. We brought back images of a Scud launcher in firing position, and secured media headlines for the Tornado GR1A on its first night of operations. On landing back at Dhahran, the Tornado was found to have a single flak hole in the top of the rudder!'

Since the Gulf conflict, a number of Tornado upgrades have taken place. The GR1B is in service with two squadrons in the maritime attack role,

having replaced the Buccaneer. The first GR4 from the mid-life update programme, was delivered to No 9 Squadron at Bruggen, Germany in April 1998. Tornado F3s are also the subject of a missile and systems upgrade, to give it AMRAAM and ASRAAM capability, until the arrival of the Eurofighter.

POWERPLANT: Two 66.80kN (15,000lb st) Turbo-Union RB199 Mk103 turbofans (GR1)
SPAN: 13.90m (45ft 7in) fully extended, 8.59m (28ft 2in) fully swept; Length: 16.71m (54ft 10in)
MAX SPEED: 2336 km/h (1452 mph)
TYPICAL ARMAMENT: GR1 – Two 27mm Mauser guns, plus warload of 9018kg (19,840lb) on three fuselage and four wing pylons; weapons include Paveway laser-guided bombs, ALARM, two AIM-9 Sidewinder SRAAMs, iron bombs or airfield/runway denial weapons; GR1B – two Sea Eagle missiles; F3 – one 27mm Mauser cannon, four underfuselage Skyflash AAMs and two AIM-9L Sidewinders on each underwing pylon
FIRST AIRCRAFT FLOWN: 14 August 1974 (IDS); 27 October 1979 (ADV)
ENTERED RAF SERVICE: July 1980 (GR1, TTTE); November 1984 (F2, No 229 OCU); April 1987 (F3, No 29 Squadron; April 1998 (GR4, No 9 Squadron); all versions except F2 still current.

LOCKHEED TRISTAR

The Tristar was purchased for the RAF for conversion as a tanker/transport, following the Falklands conflict of 1982. That campaign threw up the need to expand the tanker fleet with the impending retirement of the Victor K2. This was earlier than expected following the intensity of operations with this ageing machine in the South Atlantic. Also, the need for a long-range type for transport duties between the UK and the RAF's new base at Mount Pleasant meant there was an urgent need for a large aircraft that could be quickly converted to a tanker/passenger or tanker/freighter configuration. The Lockheed L1011 Tristar fitted this requirement, being a proven wide-bodied airliner design well suited to such a demanding military tasking.

Initially, six ex-British Airways Tristars were purchased and converted by Marshall of Cambridge to become KC1 tanker/freighters. The first was delivered to No 216 Squadron at RAF Brize Norton in August 1983, the Tristar became the heaviest aircraft – and the only wide-bodied type – in RAF service from that date.

The initial purchase of six Tristars was increased to nine by the purchase of ex-Pan American aircraft, and these were converted to C2/C2A standard, with provision for up to 265 passengers. The fleet saw service in the Gulf in 1991, when two Tristars painted in desert pink camouflage and known as Pinky and Perky were used to refuel Tornado F3 interceptors which undertook combat air patrols during the course of Operation *Desert Storm*.

Below: Following the Falklands campaign of 1982 the RAF needed additional long-range transport and flight-refuelling aircraft. This requirement was met with the purchase of second-hand TriStar airliners from British Airways and the former Pan American Airways. They were converted to tanker/passenger/freighter configuration by Marshall of Cambridge.

1983

A Tristar pilot reported on his time in the Gulf, 'The UK build-up at Dhahran in Saudi Arabia began on 9 August with the arrival of our two Tristar K1s carrying administrative and support personnel, and the F3s flew in two days later. We subsequently flew from King Khalid airfield and Muharraq, Bahrain to refuel the Tornado F3s, our main customers, on CAPs. In addition we not only passed fuel to our Jaguars and Buccaneers, but also to Canadian CF-18s, French Mirage 2000s and a variety of US Navy and Marine Corps warplanes. The C1s were involved in deploying combat aircraft to the Gulf theatre before, during and after *Desert Storm*, being able to carry heavy equipment as well as to refuel aircraft in flight.'

Left: A Tristar K1 of No 216 Squadron refuellling a Tornado GR1 during Operation *Desert Storm.*

POWERPLANT: Three 223kN (50,000lb st) Rolls-Royce RB-211-254 B4 turbofans
SPAN: 50.13m (164ft 6in); Length: 50.04m (164ft 2.5in)
MAX SPEED: 879km/h (545mph)
ACCOMMODATION: Crew of three and accommodation for up to 204 passengers
FIRST AIRCRAFT FLOWN: 16 November 1970 (L1011)
ENTERED RAF SERVICE: August 1983 (KC1, No 216 Squadron); still current.

BOEING SENTRY

The service entry of the E-3D Sentry AEW1 in 1991 came at the end of much debate and controversy that had raged since the late 1970s over the RAF's long-term airborne early warning equipment. The need to replace the elderly Shackleton AEW2s of No 8 Squadron saw the Boeing E-3, which had come into the USAF inventory in 1977, emerge as the obvious choice, being based on the exceptionally well-proven Boeing 707/C-135 airframe. However, for political and other reasons, it was decided to develop the Nimrod AEW3, with a planned entry into service in 1982.

With no operational aircraft in prospect by 1986, the Ministry of Defence cancelled the Nimrod AEW3 programme, which had been beset by problems, and ordered seven Boeing E-3s after all. Retaining the distinctive Westinghouse AN/ARY-2ODR radar system, the RAF E-3D features higher performance General Electric turbofans in enlarged cowlings, which give longer endurance and lower noise levels, added Yellow Gate ESM pods at the wingtips, and an in-flight refuelling probe above the cockpit. The windowless fuselage accommodates nine multi-purpose console screens and a data-processing

Below: The Sentry ALW1 is fitted with a flight refuelling probe so that it can extend its airborne time using the services of a Otanker aircraft.

253

1990

POWERPLANT: Four 106.9kN (24,000lb st) General Electric/SNECMA CFM-56 2A2 turbofans
SPAN: 44.42m (145ft 9in); Length: 46.61m (152ft 11in)
MAX SPEED: 855km/h (530mph)
ACCOMMODATION: Crew of five and thirteen electronics operators
FIRST AIRCRAFT FLOWN: 9 February 1972 (USAF E-3A)
ENTERED RAF SERVICE: 26 March 1991 (AEW1, No 8 Squadron); still current.

computer console. These Sentry AEW1s are amongst the most advanced airborne early warning and control system aircraft currently in service.

The RAF's Sentry AEW1s are based with Nos 8 and 23 Squadrons at RAF Waddington but detachments are deployed to overseas locations as they are declared to NATO and UN-backed campaigns. Since 1992, they have been engaged in Operation *Warden* over Northern Iraq and more recently over Bosnia for *Decisive Endeavour* and *Deliberate Guard*. From its lofty operating altitude, particularly over Europe, it can observe traffic across several countries. Sentries also regularly exercise with Tornado F3 interceptors to prevent 'adversaries' from penetrating UK airspace. Crews are also involved in long-range deployments with Tornado squadrons for overseas exercises, including visits to the Far East, Canada and South Africa.

Left: After the costly failure of the Nimrod AEW3 programme, the Ministry of Defence ordered seven Boeing E-3D Sentry airborne warning and control system aircraft to replace the RAF's veteran Shackleton AEW2s. The first of these Sentry AEW1s entered service with No 8 Squadron at RAF Waddington in July 1991.